The Inside Story
Kerry

The Inside Story
Kerry

Emily Herbert

JB

JOHN BLAKE

Published by John Blake Publishing Ltd,
3 Bramber Court, 2 Bramber Road,
London W14 9PB, England

www.johnblakepublishing.co.uk

First published in paperback in 2009

ISBN 978-1-84454-790-6

British Library Cataloguing-in-Publication Data:

A catalogue record for this book is available from the British Library.

Design by www.envydesign.co.uk

Printed in Great Britain by CPI Bookmarque, Croydon, CR0 4TD

1 3 5 7 9 10 8 6 4 2

Papers used by John Blake Publishing are natural, recyclable products made
from wood grown in sustainable forests. The manufacturing processes conform
to the environmental regulations of the country of origin.

Pictures reproduced with kind permission of Rex Features, Empics/PA Photos
and Capital Pictures.

Every attempt has been made to contact the relevant copyright-holders,
but some were unobtainable. We would be grateful if the appropriate
people could contact us.

CONTENTS

1
WHO CARES?

Kerry Katona was thirteen years old. Quietly minding her own business, she was trying to ignore the shouting going on in the background. But this was more than the usual rows between her mother Sue and Sue's violent boyfriend; this was getting quite out of control. First, the boyfriend slapped Sue viciously across the face. Then he turned on Kerry. As both women started screaming, Kerry was sure she was going to die.

'Mum and her boyfriend were rowing and he slapped her,' Kerry later recalled. 'The next thing I knew, blood spurted out. Then he turned round to face me. I saw the flash of a blade and I was convinced he was going to kill me. We managed to fend him off until the neighbours came rushing in.'

Scenes of chaos and shouting ensued as the neighbours

sought to hold him, while both women screamed for help. There had often been rows before, but this one had spiralled totally out of control and the neighbours knew that someone had to take action to protect the pretty schoolgirl and her mother and so, after some agonising, Social Services were alerted.

This was not the first time Social Services in Warrington, Cheshire, had been in touch with the Katonas. Sue had long been known to have mental problems and, although her own mother and sister helped as much as they could, there had long been concerns about her daughter Kerry's welfare. The identity of Kerry's father was and still is a mystery to her; her mother's subsequent marriage seemed, for a while, to provide some sense of stability, but it had long since broken down. Since then, there had been a succession of boyfriends, none of whom were good father or husband material and none of whom were able to provide the security both mother and daughter so desperately craved. And now Sue had found herself with a partner who seemed set on doing herself and her daughter some harm.

And this was to prove the breaking point. Sue was told by Social Services to choose between her daughter and her boyfriend. She chose the latter. 'I remember thinking, "Oh, Mum, couldn't you for once have chosen me over him?"' Kerry said. 'But I had to forgive her. No matter what she did, she was all that I had.'

Indeed, the bond between the two has always been close

2

and, in the light of Kerry's marriage breakdown, has become stronger still. Neither should Sue be judged harshly; she had a mental illness that blighted much of Kerry's childhood. But it was a harrowing time for both women and it would be some years before Kerry was old enough to make the break from her difficult background and strike out on her own.

Kerry Katona is a survivor. She's had to be. If the secret of success is an unhappy childhood, then Kerry was destined for greatness from the moment of conception, because her childhood wasn't so much unhappy as horrific. She never knew her father, and her mother's mental illness left her unable to look after her child. Kerry spent years being moved from one foster home to the next, from one refuge to another, all the while desperately seeking a stability that, as a child, she never found.

Now, of course, Kerry is one of Britain's most famous celebrities, an ex-Atomic Kitten, an erstwhile Queen of the Jungle ... and a star. But it has taken incredible strength to overcome her dreadful early years and become one of our best-loved faces. It could all have ended up very differently indeed.

'I was so down,' Kerry says. 'I wanted to jump out of windows. I wanted to die. I really did and I just kept thinking I don't know what's going to happen tomorrow. I didn't have a very good childhood but Mum had the worst childhood of all and spent it mostly in care, too. She never really knew how to love, so I lived with my aunties, my stepdad, foster parents and in care homes.' It was a very tough time, but it resulted in making Kerry tough, too. There is certainly a vulnerability about her, but it should be no surprise when she bounces back from adversity. She's had to – right from the start.

Kerry Jayne Elizabeth Katona was born on 9 September 1980 in Warrington, Cheshire, and from the very beginning it was clear there would be trouble ahead. Her mother Sue had had an affair with a married man who had other children of his own, which resulted in her falling pregnant. The affair was over by the time the pregnancy was discovered; she was determined, however, to go ahead with it.

'Susan was adamant she was going to have the baby,' said Betty Katona, Kerry's grandmother, who helped her granddaughter through some of her most difficult times, 'although her relationship had already ended when she realised she was expecting. Kerry's dad is probably kicking himself now when he sees how well his daughter has done. In a funny way, not having him around has helped Kerry – it made her want to do well and make something of her life.'

It was a brave decision on Sue's part and so she went ahead and had her child. As she was growing up, however, Kerry felt the absence of a father as she began to realise she had only one parent. Indeed, she only discovered that her father was married to someone else when she was eight and, to this day, she has no idea as to his true identity. 'I started looking at men on the street, wondering if one of them was my real dad,' she admitted. She did not, however, try to find him. 'Maybe it's because I couldn't face any more rejection,' she said.

But like so many children who do not know the full story behind their past, Kerry has clearly been marked by the experience. For a start, the yearning to know more about her background remained. 'I've never known my dad and he never got in touch,' she said wistfully on another occasion. 'But I must look like him because I'm not like my mum – she's got dark-brown hair and blue eyes and I'm blonde with dark-brown eyes.' It is a touching remark and a reminder of just how difficult her childhood was. Even today, Kerry retains a deep sense of insecurity even in her adult life as a successful performer. That said, she also has an extremely tough streak, one that has helped her to survive both her childhood and problems in her adult life.

Matters were not helped by the fact that the little family was desperately poor and frequently found themselves with nowhere they could really call home. There was never any money and the duo often had to rely on external agencies for help. 'When I was a baby, we moved around women's refuges,' Kerry recalled. 'I remember Christmas time in one of them when the Salvation Army came around with a big bag of toys.'

On another occasion, the family was so hard up they had to sell their pet parrot to buy essentials. Life was as harsh as it could be and, at that stage at least, the future seemed destined to be bleak. With disadvantages like these to overcome, it takes a will of iron to break free.

Eventually, Sue moved with her daughter to a tiny council flat, which was so small that they had to share a bed. But that did not herald the end of their problems; the years of dreadful insecurity had taken their toll and Sue's health was worsening. When Kerry was three, she made a traumatic discovery – that her mother, who was by now twenty-three, had been slashing her wrists. It was an awful discovery for a child to make, especially one so young, but Kerry, as she always did, somehow managed to cope. Indeed, she was and remains completely forgiving of her mother for all the problems she endured as a child.

'I always knew Mum loved me, but life wasn't easy for her as she was a depressive,' Kerry said in later years. 'One minute we'd be laughing and joking, the next she would be telling me she wanted to die. I found out that she'd been slashing her wrists when she once rolled up her sleeves to wash the dishes. Wrapping bandages around her wrists became a part of my life. I knew if I wasn't around, she'd be dead. That was a big responsibility for a little girl.'

As with so much in Kerry's childhood, it had a profound affect on her later years and her relationship with her mother, which is now stronger than it has ever been. There were – almost inevitably, given the circumstances – periods of near estrangement when Kerry was growing up, but behind it all was always a very deep affection and an extremely strong bond, which might in part have been promoted by the fact that, even as a very young child, it was Kerry who had to play the maternal role.

The very fact that she grew up having to look after her mother when it really should have been the other way around created an added depth to the relationship. Kerry has never criticised her mother, never blamed her for anything at all in her childhood and always maintained that she wanted to be as close to her own children as she was to her mother. In those very early days, it was Sue and Kerry against the world and, even when they were living apart, that never really changed.

When Kerry was five, her mother married Arnold Ferrier, a kind man, and who already had four children of his own. There seemed, for a short while, to be some semblance of stability in the household. Kerry was devoted to her new father and was soon calling him 'Dad'. It was the first time she had ever had a proper paternal figure in the background and someone with whom to share the burden of her mother's illness. It marked a brief period in which Kerry was allowed to be a child, without the burdens of adulthood on her very young shoulders.

Like many little girls, she was also beginning to discover a love of dressing up and playing with clothes. Indeed, for the first time, the theatrical side of her character was beginning to come to light, as she started pretending to be taking part in a wedding. 'As a child, I would run around the house pretending to be the bride and I would take my Mum's white lace tablecloth and use it as the veil,' she said.

'It was my favourite game and I always imagined it was a really spectacular, grand occasion attended by really important people.' Indeed, that grand ceremony was exactly what Kerry was going to get in years to come, when she fulfilled her childhood ambition and became the bride she had always dreamed about.

But that early happiness was not to last. Sue and Arnold split after three years, and Kerry initially stayed with her stepfather, partly because she was devoted to him and partly because of her mother's mental health problems. Sue, however, swiftly decided that she wanted her daughter to live with her and launched a custody battle, which she won. Kerry was, after all, her daughter, and she was determined to look after her herself, difficult as it so clearly was. And it was a commendable decision, made for all the right reasons, despite the problems involved.

Sadly, however, life became even more difficult for mother and daughter, with Sue choosing a series of violent boyfriends, who would turn on both her and her daughter. 'Some of Mum's boyfriends used to beat the crap out of her and me,' Kerry revealed. None of them compared to Arnold, who had been a loving and affectionate father figure to Kerry; indeed, they made life as miserable as possible for Sue and her child.

It was no life for a little girl and it was soon to get even worse. It had become obvious to everyone that Kerry simply could not continue living with her mother. Sue clearly loved her daughter, but equally was simply not capable of looking after her. And so Kerry was sent into foster care for the first time. By the age of 16, she would have lived with three different families before, with the fourth, at last finding some semblance of a caring and stable family life.

Kerry's early fostering experiences were dreadful; she did not find the foster homes loving and later said she was treated differently from the natural children of the parents she lived with. There might have been awful problems involved with living with her mother, but at least she knew that Sue loved her and wanted nothing but the best for her daughter. That was not the case with the first three foster families Kerry was sent to live with.

She never settled down into any of the families, and never found any real sense of happiness, something recognised by her husband Brian McFadden before the two split up. 'What she says to me is that her whole life people have let her down,' he said. 'She never met her dad. She had all these different foster parents and people always abandoned her or let her down.' Sadly, of course, Brian was ultimately to do the same thing himself, although in the early years he was very aware of the trauma his wife had had to live through.

One benefit from all of this suffering was that it did establish in Kerry a very strong desire to make something of her life. 'Being in Care made me even more determined to show what I was worth and that I could succeed,' Kerry said later. 'People can be judgemental about those who have been in Care, assuming they're trouble, or stupid.' It was, undeniably, a very difficult time in her life.

Neither was there much relief when she visited her mother at home, as Sue's violent, self-harming episodes continued. 'One day, Mum walked in with her wrists covered in blood. I couldn't take it,' said Kerry. 'I told her if God wanted her dead, He'd have taken her by now. Then I flung her pills at her and said, "Mum, if you're gonna do it, go ahead." It sounds horrible but it was what she needed to hear.'

Indeed, it did the trick; that was the last time Sue tried to hurt herself. But it was a terrible stage for Kerry to live through. As a child, having to inflict 'tough love' on a parent takes a maturity far beyond most people's years and, yet again, Kerry was forced to take on the parental role. Although still very young, Kerry was having to grow up fast.

The constant changes in where and with whom she lived caused problems in other ways, too. Kerry was constantly being taken out of one school and put into another – in total, she attended eight throughout her childhood – which meant that there was no continuity either in her education or in the people she met. Kerry was not naturally academic, but that side of her was never able to develop because she was forever changing from one school to another. It was hard for her to form friendships, too. Kerry has always had an outgoing, bubbly personality, but at that age children need to be in the same place for a while together in order to form firm friendships. Scarcely had Kerry had a chance to form one set of friends, than she was forced to start getting to know a new lot. All told, it's remarkable that she has emerged as unscathed as she has.

Her grandmother Betty was only too well aware of how difficult the young Kerry's life was back then. She did her best to help, but there was a limit to what even she could do. 'It was very hard for Kerry as a youngster,' she said many years later. 'She must still go over it in her mind all the time. She was a happy-go-lucky kid, but it was hard for her. Some kids are tough and she was one of them. She used to stay with me now and again. But her Mum's made up for not being able to be there for Kerry as a teenager and everything is OK between them now.'

Kerry did, in fact, also spend periods living with her mother before meeting the family that was finally going to help her, but it was the near-stabbing episode when she was thirteen that sent her back into Care, a life that she found utterly miserable. However, shortly afterwards, there was an all too rare piece of luck in a very difficult childhood.

Kerry met Fred and Margaret Woodall, an event which turned out to be a great success. Kerry went on to live with them for three years from the age of thirteen, a period that, at long last, established some stability in her life and gave her an insight into how most people lived. A tough little girl, Kerry would probably have turned out well whatever she did, but her association with the Woodalls undoubtedly gave her a boost.

'They gave me a chance in life,' she said, looking back upon her childhood. 'They and their son Paul, who is five years older than me, showed me what real family life is like.' They gave her treats, too, that many children take for granted, among them her very own bedroom and her first holiday abroad. Kerry, unsurprisingly, grew to love them as her own family, and blossomed in the time she lived in their house.

The Woodalls, who stayed in touch with their young charge after she moved out and are still very close to her – Fred gave her away at her wedding – have nothing but happy memories of the time Kerry remained in their care. They were also extremely sensitive to her particular situation – that she and her mother loved one another, but that it was simply not practical for them to live together at that stage – and gave her the space to continue her relationship with her mother, while at the same time building up her confidence and happiness. She also began to develop into a typical teenager, who sometimes had to be kept in check.

'Kerry told us that she loved her Mum and would not swap her for the world,' said Fred. 'We never asked her what she had been through and she didn't volunteer anything. But she loved her time with us and she was a joy to have. I occasionally had to tell her off for wearing skirts that were too short, but I suppose that happens in most homes. With everything she's been through and all she's achieved, Kerry's an inspiration to anyone. She's proof that anyone can make it if they want to enough.' Of course, she was also helped by having the love and support of a new family behind her, one which was determined that she should have as normal a life as possible.

They also imposed limits, something that did the young Kerry a world of good. 'Fred taught me what it is to have a strong, supportive father figure in your life,' said Kerry. 'He and Mag showed me what real family life is like, which I had never known before I met them. They taught me discipline, though I was never a naughty kid. Mag used to ground me sometimes because I was such a little entertainer. I'd always be performing for her.'

It is a great credit to the Woodalls, to Sue and to Kerry herself, that she managed to see the positive side to her experiences. In a childhood as problematic as Kerry's, the individual concerned tends either to sink or swim, and Kerry most definitely swam. Although she has spoken as an adult of her very difficult upbringing, she has never blamed her mother – rightly, as her mother was ill – and refuses to indulge in self-pity.

'I'm not one of these pessimistic people thinking "Poor me",' she said. 'I got to meet a wonderful set of foster parents. With others, there were stupid things like parents giving their foster kids the cheap Rice Krispies while their own children got the proper ones. It was horrible because I didn't know these people and kids at that age are cruel. It was lonely but you got on with it. You have to. The way I look at it, tomorrow's another day.' It's an attitude that has stood her in good stead since then. The world of showbusiness is one of the toughest in which to make a mark and the fact that Kerry learnt early on how to be able to put the past behind her and move on to new areas was to help her enormously in the years to come.

It was while she was living with the Woodalls that Kerry first began to think that a career in showbusiness might actually be feasible. Until then, such a dream would have seemed impossible – a mother suffering from depression, a poverty-stricken background and life with a string of foster parents were a very long way from the glittering career that Kerry was ultimately to make her own. 'I wanted to get into showbiz almost from the moment I could walk,' she said. 'I was always playing around in my nan's house, performing songs and dancing around.'

But Kerry was beginning to see that it was a potential way out of the life she was then living and, more than that, it began to become apparent that she had some talent for it, too. School friends began to notice that she had a flair for music and was not averse to being noticed; it was as if she was beginning to flex a set of muscles she had not previously known she'd had.

'She was always the centre of attention,' said Michelle McManus, who was in Kerry's class at Padgate High School in Warrington and who went on to be in a dance group with the soon-to-be chanteuse. 'If she could get up and sing and dance in class, she would. She saw showbiz as her way of making something of herself. With the kind of life Kerry had, things could have turned out very differently. But she had a good head on her shoulders.'

She certainly did, and was sensible enough to be able to take the opportunities that were soon to present themselves to her. And the head of music at the school agreed, calling Kerry 'a very strong performer in every way'.

As her sixteenth birthday approached, Kerry began to sense freedom. She was clearly not academic and was keen to leave school and set up on her own as soon as possible. The Woodalls had provided her with a real home and a great deal of love and understanding, but Kerry was turning into a young woman and wanted to live in her own space. But she was not, as yet, entirely clear what she was going to do. She had no formal dramatic training of any kind, and no one to advise her. It was a difficult situation, but one that began to throw up possibilities even then.

For a start, her figure had suddenly matured into that of a very curvy and desirable woman, something that could clearly be used to her advantage. But how? Kerry had no family in the world of showbusiness, no connections and no real idea about how to get into a world so far from her own. Similarly, neither her school nor the people she knew in Warrington had any idea how she should further her plans and, if truth be told, at that stage, most of them would have considered her wildly over-ambitious.

Indeed, if truth be told, Kerry would have agreed with them. She was only a few years away from stardom by this stage, unaware as she was, but even when that stardom finally came and embraced her, Kerry sometimes seemed to have trouble believing quite how far she had come, and just how successful she was. That is not surprising, given her background, but neither, given what she had been through, was the fact that she has always managed to remain down to earth. That is at least one element in the key to Kerry's popularity – a lousy childhood combined with the fact that she kept her feet on the ground when she did become successful have made her admired in many quarters. Kerry has always managed, by and large, to bring out feelings of goodwill in others.

But back then, aged sixteen in Warrington, brimming with energy and not yet sure how to use it, Kerry had no idea what to do to make her mark and so she embarked on a path that was a high risk strategy, to put it mildly. She decided that it was in glamour modelling that she would make her mark.

2

GIRL POWER

Kerry was ready to spread her wings; she had left school and she was about to take on the world. But still the question continued to haunt her — just how was she going to go about doing that? How exactly was she going to make her mark on the world?

Kerry came from a poor, underprivileged background, she had no contacts, no qualifications, she had yet to discover her particular talents and there was no obvious career path to take. And yet Kerry was determined that somehow, whatever it took, she was going to make a life for herself. She had experienced at first hand a life of poverty and unhappiness and she was resolute that her adult life was going to be different. But what was she going to do?

Her first plan was not, perhaps, the classiest of ways in which to enter showbusiness, but it had been a route chosen by plenty of famous female stars before her, and would be done by plenty more in the future. And at first, at least, it seemed to her that it was her only way to get noticed. She decided to become a glamour model. There are very few ways that someone from Kerry's background can hope to go on to bigger and brighter things without, at the least, a very good education and so, she reasoned, if she was not unattractive, then why not pick the route chosen by so many other women?

And there seemed to be no reason she shouldn't do very well at it. Kerry had, by this time, developed an extremely pretty face, combined with an extremely voluptuous body, the ideal combination for glamour work and so, unbeknown to the Woodalls, she contacted a Liverpool photographer in order to get some glamour shots taken. These were duly produced with Kerry wearing nothing but a G-string and a bright smile. Later, she would say, 'I wanted to be famous – I'm proud of what I did. And Mum always supported me in my attempts to be a topless model.'

It was typical of Kerry, in that she has always refused to apologise or be ashamed of some early activities that some people might consider a little sleazy. Indeed, those pictures would one day return to haunt her. They were not really her finest hour and, as so many famous women have also discovered, this is not a good skeleton to have in your closet. Moreover, because of her age, the pictures caused some controversy right from the start.

Had those pictures ever appeared, of course, then her life

might have been quite different. While topless modelling can lead to a good career in showbusiness – Melinda Messenger is just one celebrity who has managed to turn it to her advantage – it can equally lead in other directions and take the model down a road that would be better not travelled. As it was, the pictures, as they always do, resurfaced when Kerry had become famous, causing her a good deal of embarrassment later on. But at that time she was still extremely young, unaware of the possible pitfalls, and keen to start out on her new career.

The tide in Kerry's affairs, however, was beginning to turn. A spectacular career did indeed await her, but it was as a singer and television star, not a regular in the pages of glamour magazines. And, ironically, it was actually Kerry's former misfortune, her background in foster care, that saved her. Social workers discovered that she had posed for the pictures, and had the pictures banned because she was still technically in Care. Kerry might have felt thwarted, but in actual fact they had done her a massive favour. When the pictures eventually did surface several years later, by this time she was less keen on a topless modelling career and Kerry managed to ban them herself.

In no way daunted, Kerry continued to cast around for ways to make her mark. When she was sixteen, she moved away from the Woodalls into her own council flat, although her relationship with the family remained extremely close and, her modelling career but a distant memory before it had even started, she began to look for ways to support herself. She had her much longed-for independence but, initially at least, was not entirely sure what to do with it.

Not that she was unprepared for work. Kerry had had jobs since she was fourteen, when she had worked in a shoe shop, and so now she proved herself ready to work in any number of jobs while she became established. There was a stint as a BT sales adviser, bar work and time in a sports shop, after which she took a job working in a fish and chip shop in Warrington, The Captain's Table, to keep some money coming in. Kerry has always had a responsible attitude towards money; even in the earliest days of Atomic Kitten, she had jobs on the side, until her earning power really began to gather strength.

She was also popular wherever she went. Phil Pitt, the owner of the fish and chip shop, was pleased with his pretty new employee. 'Kerry was always popular with the lads,' he said. 'Having her work for me was good for profits.'

Kerry herself was good-humoured about it in later years. 'After closing time, the lads used to come in drunk and ask me for my number and I'd give them the number for Warrington station,' she recalled. As for her popularity, she had a different explanation. 'I could wrap a bag of chips with my eyes closed,' she said. 'I used to be very generous... I think that's why I was so popular with the customers.'

Meanwhile, she was an enthusiastic devotee of the local club scene. Kerry had been a bit of an exhibitionist in her last years at school, and she was doing the same now when she went out dancing. 'I've always been a bit of a show-off,' she admitted. 'I used to enter talent contests dancing like Michael Jackson and you could never get me off the karaoke machine. When I went to college, I didn't know what I wanted to do apart from entertaining. The chip shop gave me some extra money to keep me going.'

She did something else, too, which, like the glamour shots, could have derailed her at the outset – she began to work as a lap-dancer at the Sugar Fantasy Club in Liverpool. But Kerry's fortunes really were on the turn. What could have ended up as just another story of a girl from the wrong side of the tracks going nowhere fast, the club actually managed to provide Kerry with an opportunity. Quite apart from honing her dancing skills, which were shortly to become very useful, it got her noticed by a local record producer, which resulted in some of her earliest professional work. She was a good lap-dancer, too – she soon became one of the most popular girls in the club, earning up to £500 on a good night.

Of course, this background came to light as soon as Kerry became famous and, again, she refused to apologise or be embarrassed by it. Indeed, she took the line of a strong, independent woman. 'I was very good at it, I have to say, and, yes, it's very sexy,' she said stoutly. 'It wasn't humiliating in the slightest.' That was fortunate, as she continued with her lap-dancing in the very earliest days of Atomic Kitten, before the band really took off. 'At the time, I was living on my own and I was in Atomic Kitten, but I wasn't earning money,' she said. 'I had to do something to pay my rent. I am very proud of the fact that I was a lap-dancer.'

As Kerry became an increasingly accomplished dancer, she began to attract attention and it was when she was dancing in a club called Mr Smith's in Warrington that she had her first big break. She was approached by someone who managed a Liverpool-based dance act called The Porn Kings, which, despite the name, was utterly above board. Would she be interested in joining the act? At first, Kerry was actually rather dismissive of her new fan, but eventually agreed to meet the rest of the group the next day. The meeting went well … and Kerry's career had begun.

Indeed, The Porn Kings was an ideal outfit with whom Kerry could learn her trade. It was very much dance/techno music, but the group established quite a following, especially in Germany, and gave Kerry her first experience of performing in front of live audiences. It also enabled her to experience touring for the first time. The Porn Kings travelled across Europe and played to crowds of up to 10,000 fans, with a particularly large audience in Berlin. Word about the group was beginning to spread.

And so it was that, one night towards the end of 1998, a very famous musician was in the audience to see The Porn Kings. Andy McCluskey, who had been in the massively successful 1980s group Orchestral Manoeuvres In The Dark, had been thinking of establishing an all-girl group for some time. Given the then massive popularity of the Spice Girls and All Saints, there was clearly a huge market for that kind of music and Andy was keen to set up a group of his own.

By the time he saw Kerry dancing on stage, she had also started making connections. Just before her eighteenth birthday, she met Liz McClarnon, who had initially planned to be a lawyer, but had by now discovered her love of showbusiness, and the two of them had become firm friends. Given that their ambitions were almost identical, the two of them had set up a partnership and were already discussing ways of furthering their careers even before Andy saw Kerry dancing.

On meeting them, Andy was convinced he had found two of the girls he needed, much to the girls' great excitement. Kerry had only recently been getting used to applause as part of a large group; now there was the opportunity to become a star in her own right. They were soon joined by Heidi Range, although she was to leave before the band hit the big time, to be replaced by Natasha Hamilton. The trio were very young, even for the pop industry – Kerry and Liz were eighteen and Natasha only sixteen – but they were all determined to do whatever it took to succeed. And it wasn't as if the idea of a hugely successful all-girl group was a ridiculous fantasy – there was already a precedent.

Of all the girl bands that started in the mid to late 1990s, the Spice Girls in particular had had a phenomenal impact on the music scene and every aspiring girl band member in the country was desperate to do what the Spices had done.

What they did not perhaps realise was just how sophisticated the marketing campaign had been when launching the Spice Girls; it was therefore extremely fortunate for the new trio that they were being guided by someone who knew the music business as well as Andy McCluskey, who was under no illusions as to what had to be done.

By this time, Andy's OMD colleague Stuart Kershaw was also involved, along with Martin O'Shea. Andy and Stewart were to write the songs for the girls and Martin was to be their manager. There was, however, that most crucial of details to sort out – the name under which the band would perform. And so, as the girls started rehearsals, a search for a name was on.

Initially, the trio called themselves Honeyhead, but soon a much better alternative suggested itself. The girls had found a clothing designer, Mary Lamb, who ran a label called Automatic Kitten, which was adopted by the group. In March 1999, this was abbreviated to Atomic Kitten and the band was on its way.

Of course, by this time, Kerry, like her fellow band members, was quite wildly excited by the direction her life had taken. Despite that initial run of shop jobs and bar work, she was actually still very young by the time the band made it and was almost taken aback at the momentum with which events were now progressing. Just a few months earlier, no greater future than that with The Porn Kings had seemed to be on offer; now, there was a very real chance that she was going to become a pop star. And, little did she know it, the new group was extremely lucky. It had actually taken several years to get the Spice Girls into shape before they were let loose on the public; in the case of Kerry and her friends, the whole process lasted less than twelve months.

In fact, their very earliest movements brought to mind not the Spice Girls but Take That. Just as the boys had done almost a decade earlier, Kerry, Liz and Tash, as they were now known to each other, started to play clubs, under-18 shows and gay pride festivals, building up the foundations of a following as well as learning their trade. The men in charge knew exactly what they were aiming at. 'We have a lot on our plates if we want Atomic Kitten to surpass the Spice Girls,' said Martin. 'But the songs are great, the girls can sing and they look fantastic.' The boys also set up a record company, Engine Records, to deal with the girls; if they didn't sign to a big label, there was talk of releasing a limited edition through Engine.

But the new group was to take off – and fast. Their first really big gig was at the Paradox Club in Liverpool performing as a warm-up act, where they went down very well with an enthusiastic audience. Next was an outing at the famous Heaven club in London, where they began to arouse some interest from the music scene. Radio roadshows were to follow, culminating in an appearance at Birmingham's Gay Pride event at the end of May. The girls were definitely making a mark.

They had been busy in the studio, too – 'Right Now', 'See Ya' and 'Holiday' had all been recorded and were ready to be heard. Everyone involved was confident that it was now a case of when, rather than if, the girls became stars.

The next task was to find a big record label. With Andy, Stuart and Martin at the helm – who, between them, knew everyone there was to know in the music business – this was not a difficult task, on top of which a buzz was gathering round the girls. People were beginning to ask who their increasingly feisty girls were. And so, with some fanfare, in the summer of 1999, the girls signed with Innocent Records, a subsidiary of Virgin.

The girls were wildly excited at the news, as were their families and friends. The Woodalls, in particular, were overwhelmed; they were seeing their tough little Kerry emerge from a massively underprivileged and fraught childhood into a bona fide singer in a girl band. And it was definitely Kerry who was the dominant one of the three at that stage. Ironically, given that she was to be the first to leave, Kerry was the mouthiest of a mouthy trio. She was ecstatic that she was on the verge of the big time, and made sure everyone else shared her joy, along with almost becoming the band's de facto spokeswoman. Indeed, it was she who made an announcement once the deal had been signed.

'The songs that Andy and Stuart have written are so good that I think we can make it big,' said Kerry in her first recorded public statement, as the press began to wake up to the new singing sensation in their midst. 'Our first single, "Right Now", comes out on November 22 and we are hoping that it will reach the Top Ten. My ambition is to play one of the big festival venues because, if you do that, you know you have made it big. I'd also love to tour America and be successful over there. I didn't expect it all to happen so fast. My family and friends are still in shock.' As for Kerry herself, she had to postpone the celebrations; shortly after signing the deal, she went into hospital to have her tonsils taken out.

The buzz continued to grow. Andy and co knew that the girls had to make an instant splash once they'd arrived on the scene, and so were promoting them as heavily as they could. Another Atomic Kitten song, 'Something Spooky', was to be used as the theme tune for the children's television show *Belfry Witches*, which started that September. The girls signed up to support 911 during their UK tour that September and they also agreed to appear at the Liscard Show in Wallasey on the August Bank Holiday.

The girls were well aware what an opportunity awaited them and happily complied with all their mentors' demands. The trick was to get as much exposure as possible and establish themselves as rapidly as possible almost before anyone realised they had arrived. And it was not proving difficult. The girls' natural exuberance and their strong personalities were both winning them friends and making a mark; people were remembering them, and liking them, too.

By October 1999, plans were well advanced to launch the Kittens proper on the world stage. They had spent the summer building up a following, learning their trade and creating that all-important buzz that is absolutely crucial when launching a new pop act. It had been decided that their début single was to be 'Right Now', so Andy and his team, determined to leave absolutely nothing to chance, had hired Absolute to mix the instrumentals. It showed just how seriously everyone was taking this new venture; Absolute had worked with the Spice Girls and, more latterly, with a solo Geri Halliwell. Atomic Kitten was quite clearly to be pitched at the big league.

Meanwhile, the serious marketing that involves launching a new group was being employed behind the scenes. The cable TV music show *The Box* had been given a promo video of 'Right Now' and had given their assurance that it would be played at least 12 times a day. Staff at the channel were said to be seriously impressed by the new band. The girls were also doing their bit; they were giving interviews to assorted newspapers and the magazines *Smash Hits* and *TV Hits*, as well as appearing on the *Big Breakfast* and *Live and Kicking*. Further appearances followed on *This Morning*.

Work on the début album, due for release early the following year, was also under way; it was to appear first in Japan, where the girls had already amassed quite a following. Indeed, they already had a sponsorship deal for a chocolate bar in the Far East.

Everyone involved was very canny about how best to show off the new team. One of Atomic Kitten's many appearances was at none other than Kerry's old stomping ground – Padgate High School. The trio put on a lunchtime performance of 'Right Now', 'See Ya' and 'Big Country', all of which enthralled the current pupils of the school. Kerry was delighted. 'It was amazing – we went down really well,' she said. 'It was just like being back at school and it felt so good to see everybody enjoying something I had done.'

Kerry was sure she knew the secret of their success. 'We're so in your face,' she said. 'We're real. We're not like, "Hi, our record company said we have to wear these clothes and have to be in bed by eight o'clock." We're not going to pretend we're all sweet and innocent, 'cos no one's sweet and innocent.' While the band might have been manufactured to a certain degree, it had a freshness few of the others seemed to capture. But even the ever-optimistic Kerry couldn't really have foreseen what was about to happen. The three girls – Atomic Kitten – were about to experience success beyond their wildest dreams.

By November, excitement was really beginning to mount. 'Right Now', which had not yet been released, was getting plenty of air play from local radio stations, again a crucial element in making the single a success. It had already caused a controversy, too, something that has never been known to harm record sales – the appearance on *Live and Kicking* had been briefly postponed as the lyrics of the single were deemed too raunchy for young ears. The problem was resolved when the girls agreed to sing 'See Ya' instead. They were also recruited to turn on the Christmas lights in Edinburgh, Chester and, of course, Liverpool; success now seemed assured.

And the work was beginning to pay off. By mid-November, the single had been playlisted by Radio 1; their promo CD had also made it to number 15 in the *Music Week* dance chart, a very respectable showing, given the single hadn't even been released yet. The girls were beside themselves with what they had achieved, but at the same time it was very hard work. The single was going to be released all over Europe, which meant they were appearing on Continental television as well as the domestic channels, on top of which they were scheduled to visit Japan again by the end of the year. It was heady stuff for all three of them, but especially for Kerry. Until recently, as she herself pointed out, before all this began, she had hardly ever been abroad at all.

D–Day was 25 November 1999. It was actually seen as a high-risk strategy to launch a début single at this time of the year, given that competition is extremely strong for a Christmas Number One, and so all the more established acts – and some surprises – tend to release a new record in late November. However, it worked. 'Right Now' sold 30,000 copies in its first week, reaching number 10 in the charts. It didn't quite match the Spice Girls a couple of years earlier, but it was quite enough to make a big impact and reassure Virgin Records – who had also been the Spice Girls label – that they definitely had another winner on their hands.

Kerry could scarcely believe everything that was happening to her. The launch of the record took place at Andy's Records in Warrington, allowing her the chance to see her mother for the first time in ages. 'It's all been a mad whirl – I can't believe our single's finally out!' she said. 'Today is the first time I've seen my mother in months. We did an interview on Radio 1 today where we could play a record of our choice – Liz chose "Mama" by the Spice Girls as a tribute to all our parents and I just burst into tears.'

Of course, Kerry herself was well aware that they were seen in some quarters as potential rivals to their illustrious forebears. 'Everyone compares us to the Spice Girls, which is a real honour, but nobody could ever be them – they opened up the world of pop for bands like us and introduced girl power,' she said. In actual fact, not only were the Spice Girls themselves on the verge of imploding, but Atomic Kitten were going to last the course. They were also loving every minute of it. 'It's amazing – I've already been to Japan and Ireland and next year we're off to Italy and South-East Asia,' said Kerry. 'I'd only been abroad twice before now and that was to Spain.'

On the day the single actually entered the charts, the girls celebrated by playing at Liverpool's Anfield football ground. 'We played at half-time and I kept expecting to hear chants like, "Get your kit off for the boys!"' said Kerry. 'But, actually, the crowd were really nice and supportive. Liverpool were playing Sheffield Wednesday on the day and Tash thought they were called Ashfield Wednesday. And that's what she called them on live radio! Obviously, we've never let her live it down.'

In the event, the single stayed in the charts for eight weeks, which would have been a major achievement at any time of the year and was particularly so in the run up to Christmas. By the time the new Millennium had been seen in, Atomic Kitten, who six months previously had been complete unknowns, were bona fide established stars. The band who did manage the Number One slot that year, incidentally, was an Irish outfit called Westlife. But more of them anon.

The girls were coping with their new lives like true professionals. The three of them gave an interview early in 2000, in which they were more than able to hold their own. 'We're not pretending to be something we're not,' said Kerry firmly. 'Half these girl bands or manufactured bands get signed up and then they get changed, the record company says this is how you've got to be, whereas we make the rules up and we break them as we go along.'

If truth be told, that was remarkably similar to early Spice Girls pronouncements. And there was another hark back to the Spices when the *Sun* newspaper gave them nicknames – Natasha was Ginger Kitten, Fluffy Kitten was Liz's moniker and the Sex Kitten attribute went to Kerry.

Unlike the Spice Girls' nicknames, however, they never really caught on.

Natasha was equally feisty, becoming enraged when it was suggested that Atomic Kitten itself could be accused of being a manufactured band. 'Accuse?' she cried. 'I wouldn't say it was a matter of accusing us, I would just say that it was a matter of their opinion. If people want to think we're manufactured, then that is up to them. Everyone's manufactured in that someone puts money into you, someone's got to sign you and it is their money that you're using. If people can be bothered reading the papers and read what we say in interviews, then they'll know we're not manufactured. We got signed when our album was already done, it's all been ours. It's not like they've come in and given us songs, they've all been ours from the beginning. We're nobody's puppets.'

Indeed, the trio was determined to present themselves as normal girls next door. 'That's why we appeal to a lot of our fans,' said Natasha. 'They look at us and say, "That's me! I do that!" We went to the première of *The Beach* and we were bouncing up and down, going, "Ole, ole, ole, ole" and I overheard a girl saying, "Look, everyone else is being dead posh and they're being, like, mental." We're just us, we don't put an act on for nobody, we're just typical teenagers.'

It was true, they were typical teenagers who were making quite an impact on the world, although not everything about their lives was typical, and there was a price to pay as well – no boyfriends. 'You don't get the chance to have a boyfriend,' said Natasha ruefully, 'because you don't have the chance to get to know them. You can have a date with someone, but then you don't get to see them for three weeks, and then it's maybe for an hour and you don't know if they like you because of what you're doing or because of who you are.'

It was a situation all three were prepared to accept for the time being, however, and, in truth, it was a situation which wasn't going to last long. There was also more at stake now, as well. Kerry continued to attract the most attention, while she herself was well aware of her motives behind joining the band. 'I'm in this for personal reasons,' she said. 'I was brought up in Care and I want to prove to myself that it doesn't matter who you are or what kind of background you are from, everybody is special. I want to show to myself and to kids out there who are in Care or whose parents are divorced or whatever, things can get better, I am living proof that it can be done. I've never had money, and I've never needed it, so I'm certainly not in it for the money … although fame is pretty cool as well.'

In March 2000, the next single, 'See Ya', came out. It did even better than the first and got to number 6 in the charts. Again, canny marketing played a big role; the song had previously been heard in the films *Thomas the Tank Engine and Friends* and *Bring It On*. Now that the single itself had been released, it was also being used as the soundtrack to Fiat's advertising campaigns in France and Italy, which did its popularity (and amount of airplay time) no harm at all.

The girls were also touring, and played in front of thousands at Wembley, again a sign of their new-found prowess. 'The whole tour has been fantastic,' said an enthusiastic Kerry. 'We've been getting on really well and hanging out together. It's still all very new to us but we don't get nervous – just excited. We've been enjoying every minute of it.' Neither was she letting it go to her head. 'Being put into Care was probably the best thing that ever happened to me,' she said, explaining that it helped keep her feet on the ground. 'I haven't had a sheltered upbringing and it has made me realise you have to make your own way in life. It's also taught me to enjoy every moment. Atomic Kitten will never be stuck up. We're just three girls out to have fun.'

But there was something else on Kerry's mind, too, for, young as she was, she had already met the man she was sure was going to be the right one for her. His name was Bryan McFadden.

3

PLAYING IT COOL

Bryan McFadden was born on 12 April 1980 into an Irish, middle-class family, something he once described as 'straight out of *The Partridge Family*'. Like Kerry, Bryan was a singer, in his case with the massively successful band Westlife. It was quite a step up in the world; he had once had a job in McDonald's, earning £150 a week.

Westlife had originally come about after its three founding members – Kian Egan, Shane Filan and Mark Feehily – all from Sligo in Ireland, had taken part in a local production of the musical *Grease*. The three performed so well that they were encouraged to form their own band and so, joined by three other acting friends, they set up an outfit called IOU, which was later changed to Westside.

As with the Atomic Kittens, success came quickly. Shane and Mark wrote a song called 'Together Girl Forever', made a demo tape of it and sent it to Louis Walsh, who had been the manager of the boy band Boyzone and who was currently looking for a new band to take their place. He liked their sound and signed them up to support the US band Backstreet Boys when they played Dublin, after which there was a change in the line-up. Three of the original members departed and Bryan and Nicky Byrne, both from Dublin, joined the group.

In February 1999, just as the Kittens were slowly beginning to emerge, they held a showcase at London's Café de Paris. Another name change shortly ensued, this time to Westlife, after they'd heard several US outfits were already called Westside. Their début release in May that year, 'Swear It Again', went straight to Number One; so did their four subsequent singles, something that made musical history.

Bryan and Kerry actually met in August 1999 when the Kittens and Westlife did a *Smash Hits* tour together and, for him, at least, it was love at first sight. 'He was standing outside a lift,' said Kerry later, recalling the first time she set eyes on him. 'He was in a black polo neck and he had long, floppy hair. I remember looking up really high at him, because he's tall and I'm quite little.'

'I heard the lift go "Ding", the doors opening and this girl in a bomber jacket and bog woolly boots ran out,' added Bryan. 'I heard her chatting and I turned round and she came up to me.'

'Being dead cheeky, I went up to him and said, "Hiya!

I'm Kerry from Atomic Kitten and my mate Liz is a really big fan of Westlife." He looked at me really weird.'

On another occasion, Kerry joked that she hadn't initially recognised him. 'I met him just before Christmas 1999,' Kerry said later. 'I didn't have a clue who he was. Then I found out how famous and wealthy he was, and I thought, "He's just the man for me."'

Indeed, Bryan had to work quite hard to get Kerry to agree to go out with him. 'Bryan asked me out five times on the night we met,' she revealed. 'But I told him that just because he was in a boy band didn't mean that he had what it takes to go out with me. But he was very caring and very sensitive and he made me laugh a lot.'

'It's funny, all the guys in the band had asked her out,' Bryan said, 'and so I knew she was going to say no because she'd said no to all the others.'

As it happened, the two became friends before anything started properly between them. 'Two weeks later, having got to know each other, we ended up having our first kiss,' Kerry revealed. 'We were in the hotel having this conversation. Most guys would be pitching you with their eyes, but Bryan sat down and listened. He was so funny and he made me laugh. That was it. We had our first kiss ... and then we lost touch.'

'Even though we'd both had too much to drink, I knew the first time I kissed Kerry that there was something there,' said Bryan. 'But the next day, sadly, she left with Atomic Kitten for Japan.'

Leaving for Japan was something Kerry was doing quite regularly at that stage. It was more than likely, though, that the two of them would meet up again, given that they played the same sort of gigs and, indeed, they did, that November. 'Our bands went on another tour and we just started seeing each other as friends,' said Kerry. 'I was single and I wasn't looking for a relationship. I knew Bryan was with somebody else by this time.

'Even so, we were getting on really well, flirting with each other and everything. Our bands then went to a party in Glasgow, but the girls in Atomic Kitten didn't have any spare time for boys. I really liked Bryan, but I thought, "No, he's not interested in me because he's with somebody else." And then at one point during the party, he said, "I really like you." I said, "Well, you've got a girlfriend ... the ball's in your court."'

'The girl I was with was nice, but I knew the minute I sat down and talked to Kerry that she was the one I wanted,' said Bryan. 'I left the party straight after that and finished with my girlfriend.'

By this time, the attraction was absolutely mutual. 'I thought she was wild, nuts, a real party animal,' said Bryan. 'To be honest with you – and she's going to hate me for saying this – I thought she was going to be a dumb blonde. But then I sat and talked to her and realised how wrong I was, and how deep and intellectual she was and is. Funny, as well.'

Kerry was equally enthused about her new boyfriend. 'I

tend not to trust people, but I trusted Bryan from the start,' she said. 'I could tell he really loved me. He'd get to bed at two in the morning from filming, and he'd have to be up for five o'clock, but he'd walk from his hotel to my hotel just to see me for two hours, and he'd arrange a big breakfast for us. No boyfriend had ever done anything like that for me before.'

Now that the relationship had finally begun, it quickly became extremely serious. 'He proposed to me after just three weeks and I knew he was the one – he's the most genuine, down-to-earth person I've met in the music business and he's so caring and loving,' Kerry said. Proposal or not, of course, it was some time before the two were to become openly engaged. Indeed, it was some time before they were even openly a couple; for both their sakes, the relationship stayed very much in the shadows for many months to come.

Bryan later recalled that he first realised he wanted to marry Kerry when she broke her coccyx that December. Kerry remembered it as a turning point, too. 'I was due to see the doctors in London and I was really nervous about it as I checked into the hotel,' she said. 'As I got there, I could hardly walk. Bryan gave me these pyjamas, which he told me to change into after he'd given me a wash. He put me in bed and covered me up. It was then that we both knew we were meant for each other.'

Despite being in such a serious relationship, however, Bryan and Kerry let it slip out that while they might have briefly dated, by now they were merely good friends. They had no option other than to do so. Both were to reveal later that both sets of record labels were not that delighted at the turn of events, given that both stars were more marketable if they were single, and so they played everything down. Only their very closest family and friends knew what was really going on behind the scenes – that they had actually decided to get married – and it was to be a long time before the engagement became public knowledge.

By April, Atomic Kitten were on tour as the support band for Steps, something that took them to Dublin. But Kerry was keen to scotch any rumours that she and Bryan were back together. 'Bryan and I are not together and I've been far too busy for boys,' she said firmly. 'When we were going out, though, I never got any hassle from Westlife fans – they were fantastic and our fans were brilliant as well. I was pretty made up with it actually, but unfortunately he's busy and I'm busy. We're still friends, though. I know a few people in Ireland so while I'm here I'll probably go out and see a few friends, have a few drinks, have some *craic* as they say in Ireland.'

But it was not impossible to be both the member of a band and to have a relationship, as none other than Kerry's fellow Atomic Kitten was to prove. In June 2000, Liz became engaged to her childhood sweetheart, a 23-year-old warehouse supervisor called Tom Hibbs, whom she had met when she was just twelve. 'We're not going to get married just yet – I think I'm a bit too young for that – but it's nice to be engaged,' she said. 'I have liked him since I was twelve and we were best mates before we started seeing each other. Our relationship is great – I love him so much.'

And on the thorny subject of managing to combine both business and pleasure, she was adamant that it could be done. 'I laugh when I hear famous people say they can't have a relationship because they are in showbiz and things are so hectic,' she said. 'If you want it to work, it will work. Being in a band hasn't affected our relationship or how I feel about Tommy. It just means it can get expensive because of all the travelling and the phone calls, but neither of us wants to split.' So it seemed that a genuinely loving and long-lasting relationship was possible after all.

Kerry at this stage seemed to be in an increasingly playful mood. For a start, she claimed to have a crush on Rod Stewart. 'I think he is incredibly sexy and I love his songs,' she said. 'The first thing I'll say when I meet him is, "If you think I'm sexy, do you want my body?" Because I'm blonde I could be in with a chance. I can't wait for us to become an item. I'm determined to make it happen.' Hardly pausing for breath, she was then seen out with Dan Corsi, the singer from Northern Line.

Bryan also appeared to be casting around for a new romance, in his case with the pop star Billie Piper, who had recently split from her long-term boyfriend Ritchie Neville. 'I've dated some girls in the pop business and it hasn't worked out because of my busy schedule,' he remarked. 'But I'd definitely like to go out with Billie. She's a great-looking girl with a nice personality. I've got her phone number, so I'll call her soon. Right now we are good friends. We frequently bump into each other at music events, but if the chemistry was right, I'd like it to be more.' As an item, Kerry and Bryan seemed to be a thing of the past – until, that is, they were caught kissing at a party.

It can't have been easy for them, not least because both were now the focus of so much attention. Apart, they made good headline material, but together, as Victoria Adams and David Beckham had already discovered, they were sensational. Both were young and attractive, so they had both – but especially Bryan – quickly become the target for over-enthusiastic fans. Indeed, a story emerged that when Bryan was touring in Florida, he opened his hotel door to find two naked 18-year-old girls sprawled out on the bed waiting for him. Bryan promptly called security.

'It's the biggest shock I've had so far in Westlife, although it may seem funny to some people,' he said. 'At the end of the day, they didn't mean any harm. I think they just got a bit carried away.' A spokeswoman for the band confirmed that this is what had happened. 'He doesn't know how the girls got in. It must have been quite scary,' she said. 'Most hot-blooded men would take longer to call security, but Bryan did the right thing immediately. Westlife have fans throwing themselves at them, so these two girls wouldn't have interested Bryan. The rest of the lads had a good laugh about it and found it very funny.'

As for the girls themselves, they asked if they could stay,

but were escorted from the premises by security. Rather more seriously, they had also been seen going through Bryan's address book. 'One of them was leafing through my phone diary and writing down numbers,' said Bryan. 'I've had to ring loads of people, including Mariah Carey and Ronan Keating, to tell them their phone numbers may have been discovered by the girls.'

There was some ribaldry, in the wake of that, about men who get alarmed by finding naked women in their bedroom, but security was becoming a serious issue for both Westlife and Atomic Kitten. The latter had played at Tranmere Football Club in June and were subjected to an attempted attack. A man pretending to know them had tried to get close to the girls. 'When we played at Tranmere, this guy was trying to get it on with security, making out he was one of our boyfriends and trying to get backstage,' said Kerry. 'He didn't get in but they gave us a police escort out of the show just in case he did anything. And he was there saying, "I'll be back." It was pretty scary – I hope he doesn't come back.' Shortly afterwards, it emerged that they were receiving strange letters. 'We have been getting letters like you see in the movies with the words cut out of newspapers, which is weird,' Kerry said.

Meanwhile, the Kittens' star continued to soar in the Far East. By the middle of the year, they had become Japan's biggest new international act, judged both by their profile and by the sales of their records. But Japan was not alone in its admiration of the girls; their following in the Orient had become so huge that MTV put them at the forefront of MTV Asia's new campaign, which launched in June. Not content with that, they performed at the MTV Asia Awards alongside Alanis Morissette and Aqua, a performance that was seen by 675 million people.

As Kerry's fame grew, it was inevitable that there was an increased interest in her past life. She had been quite open about her years in Care, but was rather less pleased when her early foray into topless modelling came to light. Pictures emerged in some of the papers, along with reports about the fact that she'd been a lap-dancer. She took it in fairly good spirit, although refusing, as always, to apologise. Instead, she talked quite openly about her past.

'I knew one day they would probably get out but, when it came to the crunch, I was really scared about the reaction,' she said. 'I'd done them at the age of sixteen for an older male audience. I didn't know then that I'd be in Atomic Kitten. I didn't know I would be a role model for young girls and I kept thinking that a kid would look at them and think either, "This is what I should do," or, "She shouldn't be doing that, she's a slut." But I'm not at all. I was in a few foster homes and by then I was sixteen, living on my own in a flat and somehow I had to get by. I had the bust, I wanted to be famous and that's how I saw I could do it at that time. And I enjoyed modelling.'

Indeed, she put her background – or the Care part of it, at least – to good use, as Atomic Kitten leant their support to Nickelodeon's The Big Help, a project that encouraged young people to help others in the community. 'I spent time with different families in London and Warrington. Now it's good to be able to give something back,' she said, and the other Kittens were equally keen. 'The good thing is everyone can help in some way, even if it's something small like cleaning your neighbour's car,' said Natasha. The Kittens were clearly willing to do their bit.

But there was little time to hang about. By August that year, they had visited Japan – where they remained an absolutely huge success – five times and were now set for a sixth visit, which would be part of a six-week tour of Japan, Malaysia, Taiwan, Indonesia and Thailand. 'This is our sixth trip to Japan this year,' said Natasha. 'We've recorded a version of the Monkees hit 'Daydream Believer' for a Japanese film and we're going to the première.' They were also beginning to enjoy their new-found wealth. 'Kerry and I are moving to London soon, so we'll rent a nice flat,' Natasha added. 'And I'd love to buy my mum and dad a house.'

But the work was also taking its toll. Once out in Thailand, all three girls came down with various afflictions, starting with Natasha, who was rushed to the Bumrungrad hospital in Bangkok after contracting bronchitis. The other two girls were forced to play a gig in the city's CM Squared nightclub without her.

Liz was next. Just before she was due to give an interview with Bangkok's 95.5 FMX radio station, she developed an acute earache and had to return to her hotel.

Kerry soldiered on, cheerfully telling the presenter that the band might have developed alcohol poisoning after a night in the city's bars, but she, too, was not at her best and it soon emerged she had the 'flu. Helen Knox, who was managing the band on their tour, was good-natured about it. 'Kerry's to blame!' she said. 'She's given us all a bug. But the Kittens will troop on. They've been resting and gobbling antibiotics and now we're off to Taiwan.'

It was an exhausting schedule, however, and one that was bound to take its toll. And then Kerry had an additional burden – she was still keeping the relationship with Bryan a secret, although rumours were beginning to circulate about the real state of affairs. And, of course, she couldn't spend that much time with her boyfriend. Westlife and Atomic Kitten were both frantically busy just about all the time.

On their return to Britain, though, Kerry was clearly back on form. She was escorted to a pop festival by one mystery admirer, only to spend the rest of the evening with one Bryan McFadden, who also happened to be there. The real nature of their relationship was becoming increasingly clear, not least because, on spotting one another, they then disappeared for a good ten minutes. The chemistry between them was obvious to onlookers, too. It is very difficult to hide really strong feelings about another person and, increasingly, Kerry and Bryan didn't want to.

Indeed, they were finally ready to tell the truth, that they had actually been a couple for nearly a year, a secret that came out when they were spotted on holiday on the beach together in Gran Canaria. The subsequent pictures made the headlines, and the pop world's worst-kept secret was finally out – the two 19-year-old stars were an item.

'Bryan is one of the most important things in my life and we're so happy together,' said Kerry, clearly relieved that she could at last tell her news. 'He makes me laugh and I feel on top of the world.' Indeed, she had even had a tattoo done in honour of Bryan. 'I had it done about three weeks ago while we were in Japan,' she said. 'It hurt but I did it for Bryan.'

Bryan was equally effusive about his girlfriend. 'I love Kerry,' he said. 'She is the best thing in the world. We have such a great time together. We have both got really mad schedules so when we get to spend some time to ourselves, it's very valuable.'

Time together was at a premium, though, as work continued for both; Westlife was just about to release a cover version of the Phil Collins song 'Against All Odds', while Atomic Kitten was bringing out 'Follow Me'. Westlife had also been working on their second album entitled *Coast to Coast* – which, ironically enough, was going up against the Spice Girls – and the band felt it was better than their first, *Westlife*. 'It's a lot more tempo on this album, more of a big summer feel, but we still have the wintry ballads,' said Bryan. 'There's a few up-tempos as well, like the Celine Dion-type of up-tempos. It's not like the stomp of Backstreet Boys. We're not worried. In our opinion, the songs on the album are better than on the first album.' It had something else, as well – on the CD sleeve, there was a special message from Bryan to Kerry: 'My angel, thanks for changing me, I love you, sweetheart.'

Bryan was beginning to feel the strain, though; three members of Westlife – Bryan included – had had to be flown home from their tour over the summer as they were too exhausted to carry on, and now there was a heavy promotional schedule ahead. 'There are times I regret what we do,' he said. 'Sometimes, you wish you'd never done this, you just want to go home. I don't know if it's worth all the sacrifices, but then I think about it and realise I couldn't get a normal job in Ireland today because of our success. It would be impossible, not even at McDonald's. I miss just having a regular life – getting up at 8.00am and coming home again in the evening and being free to do what you want. It would be great not to have any tie-ins. Most people can take a day off – we can't. They can get out and get drunk on a Saturday night, but we can't. Our lives are controlled.'

Of his collapse during the summer, he said, 'We had been going straight for three months and it just took its toll. I had to go home for a couple of days. I was just really, really tired. I couldn't face another day. I didn't want to go on another plane, I just wanted to go home. The irony was I had to go on a plane to go home. It can get very stressful.

The getting up, getting on planes, changing countries and cities all the time. It's exciting for the first week, but the rest is awful.'

His girlfriend was finding life equally stressful. 'Being in the public eye has made me so paranoid, I can't go out without a couple of drinks,' she said. 'Sometimes, I even go down to my mum's local, which is full of dodgy characters, where I won't get recognised. Then, after a couple, I feel ready to face the world again.'

With both so overstretched and exhausted, it was only a matter of time before the two reached breaking point (albeit temporarily) and so it happened that Kerry and Bryan had a huge row in public in September 2000. Atomic Kitten, Westlife and the singer Louise had all been booked to appear at a show staged by TV firm FIP's Music 2000 gig at the Millennium Dome. Atomic Kitten had to pull out at the last minute, as Liz's mother had to go to hospital. Kerry and Natasha went along anyway. 'We're gutted we had to pull out at such short notice,' said Kerry. 'Me and Natasha offered to sing anyway.' But trouble brewed when Kerry discovered Bryan chatting happily to two other girls. An onlooker revealed what happened next. 'Kerry and Bryan had been all over each other all day, kissing and cuddling,' he said. 'But when Westlife came off stage, Bryan made a beeline for these two other girls, totally ignoring Kerry. Understandably, she was annoyed and stormed out to her dressing room. Bryan ran after her and you could hear the pair of them screaming and swearing at each other. It wasn't hard to recognise them – he's got a broad Irish accent and she's a Scouser. She was shouting, "You don't understand," and he was screaming, "Stop being so fucking stupid." Next thing we knew, Kerry reappeared in a skimpy pink dress.'

Indeed, she had done so to appear in a fashion show in London's elegant Sanderson Hotel, where the two Kittens were reunited with Westlife. Kerry and Bryan appeared to make up and continued on to the fashionable Met Bar, but neither looked ecstatic. The frenetic lifestyle was clearly taking its toll.

But, keen to put the row behind them, the two lost no time in very publicly declaring their love for one another. They had already admitted that they were an item; now they gave a full interview about their relationship. 'I'm going out with Bryan,' said Kerry. 'I have been since last November. I'm really sorry if Westlife fans are upset, but I'm only human and I can't help who I fall in love with. I'm just like them. When I go home at night, I want someone to say "Hello" and hold me when I'm sad. Bryan's that person.'

Bryan was more effusive still. 'It's true,' he said. 'Kerry and I are going out and we have been for about a year. I fell for her the first time I met her. At first, Kerry didn't know who Westlife were and it took a while to get her to go out with me. Our relationship is the most solid thing in my life. She's the most important person in my life and she's the best thing ever to happen to me. First of all, I never told anyone. The rest of the guys in the band didn't even know. Kerry and I wanted to keep our personal lives personal. We were seen out a few times but we said we were just friends because we didn't want people prying into our lives.' And as if to confirm the depth of his feelings, Bryan also lavished gifts upon Kerry, one of which was a Mercedes E320.

But like any celebrity couple, they were soon the focus of intensive speculation. After the row at the Dome, another story emerged about another row, this time suggesting Bryan had been flirting with another woman at the London nightclub GAY. Bryan was livid and determined to put the story to rest. 'I want to set the record straight,' he said. 'Our relationship is stronger than ever, I love Kerry with all my heart and we haven't had any arguments. The stories claiming that our relationship has hit stormy waters were very hurtful. Only last week I bought her a Mercedes.

'Everything between us is great. When we're together, I'm the happiest man in the world. I can't think why these people feel the need to make up rubbish about us. I wasn't flirting with anyone at any clubs. I wouldn't jeopardise my relationship with Kerry – it wouldn't be worth it.

'It's important to me that people back home know the truth because every day they are being fed stories that we have split up. Kerry is very upset by them, too. After a while, you learn to tolerate lies in the press, but this is ridiculous. Far from falling out, Kerry and I are stronger as a couple than ever. She was absolutely thrilled when I bought her the car. It isn't a flash-in-the-pan, showbiz romance.

'We have been close together for a long time now. She has a great personality and is the kindest person in the world. We don't go out to that many showbiz parties together because we prefer to spend quality time with each other when we get the chance.'

It was the downside of fame, as the two were now discovering, but the couple were clearly besotted with each other, while Kerry could scarcely believe the change in her circumstances. She had come a very long way from being that little girl in foster care.

Indeed, over the next few years, her life was to change again and again. At the time of writing, Kerry is still only in her mid-twenties, but has already had a number of careers, as well as fame on several different continents, and has had to cope with a number of massive upheavals in her life. Her childhood stood her in good stead; Kerry might look fragile, but she's a fighter and has come through each battle stronger still.

For now, she was enjoying her life as a pop star, which was beginning to produce some degree of security not only for her but also for Sue; as soon as she was able, Kerry began to look after her mother's wellbeing. And, of course, above all, she was enjoying being with Bryan. The two were generating huge amounts of goodwill, and just as Kerry's band had frequently been compared to the Spice Girls, so she now found herself being compared to Victoria

Beckham. Kerry and Bryan may not have been entirely the next Posh and Becks, but they were young, attractive and in love, a combination the public found enthralling. And both were to go to greater heights still. A very exciting time for both of them now lay ahead.

4

CAT LOVER

Kerry really was deliriously happy. At just 19, she was successful, the band was going from one success to the next and, above all, of course, she had Bryan. She had told him everything about her past and it didn't matter one jot. Bryan loved her for what she was and didn't care about the more difficult episodes in her life before Atomic Kitten. 'I am madly in love,' she said. 'I have never been in love like this before. He knows my life story, everything I've done and he has stuck by me. He knows about the topless modelling I've done but he doesn't care about that. He knows that I've been in foster homes and he is looking after me. He is my life.'

It was the first time Kerry had experienced a relationship like the one she had with Bryan and, quite apart from the happiness it brought her, it made her feel secure. It also provided a very good foil to the downside – for it does exist – of celebrity. The two were both extremely young and both were members of wildly successful bands. Both were in the process of going from having little or no money to some degree of wealth, a situation that can be difficult if there is no one in the background to keep your feet on the ground. But if you can share that experience with someone who is going through exactly the same thing, then, clearly, it will both ease the external pressures and strengthen the internal bond.

Indeed, now that the secret was out, Kerry and Bryan could barely bring themselves to stop talking about one another. 'We didn't hide anything – we just tried not to get seen out together,' chortled Kerry. 'A lot of fans knew anyway – particularly the ones in Ireland as we spent a lot of time there, but they were great about it. But when anyone asked us, we said we were just friends. I didn't want to be questioned all the time about him. I wanted Atomic Kitten to get recognised on their own without me getting loads of press just because I was with Bryan.

'I thought Natasha and Liz would get fed up with it and we all wanted Atomic Kitten to be established on our own merits. It was important that everyone got to know our personalities first and realised I'm not stealing Bryan away from the fans. It's just that I can't help who I love. But I'm glad now because, before, we couldn't go out together so we ended up being stuck inside hotel rooms. We didn't decide to do this. But we were all on holiday – Bryan, me, my mum, Natasha, her mum and dad and her little sister. And people recognised us and got photos of us. But we had a great time anyway – it was my mum's first time abroad so that was great.'

That emphasis on not stealing Bryan away was important. The music industry much prefers its young and attractive menfolk to be unattached, for the simple reason that it will encourage teenage female fantasies about the singers, which in turn will lead to increased record sales, something Westlife's management was obviously keen to encourage. On top of that, pop stars' girlfriends themselves sometimes come in for hostility, a situation Kerry – and Atomic Kitten's management – clearly wished to avoid. So a teen romance that was deepening into a serious relationship was not, as it would have been for most people, just a matter of celebration; it was also a tricky diplomatic situation that had to be handled with kid gloves.

And glad as they might have been that the secret was out, increased press coverage created tensions, too. Like Bryan, Kerry admitted to getting very annoyed about reports that they'd been arguing. 'One night we had a few beers and a great laugh and went home,' she recalled. 'The next day, my manager phoned at around 10.00pm to ask if Bryan and I had been rowing. We couldn't wait to see the paper as it was a mystery to us and, at the beginning, we thought it was funny.

'But as we read on, we thought, "This isn't on and it's not fair." And these stories are getting really annoying. It's upsetting because, once they're published, my mum is on the phone to me and Bryan's mum is on the phone to him asking if we've been fighting. We never have, so now they're taking what they read with a pinch of salt.'

On the whole, though, Kerry and Bryan knew how to play the game. Their continuing popularity depended on constant press coverage and both were realistic enough to know that they had to put up with a certain amount of the negative in order to get the positive.

Of course, beyond the specific problems involved in being a pop star came the rituals involved in any relationship, not least meeting the parents. In this case, everyone involved got on, much to Kerry's relief. There was also the issue of where everyone would stay when the families got together; Kerry was to buy her mother a nice house, but this was still in the fairly early days of her fame and increased wealth and she hadn't yet been able to do so. Not that that bothered her; as ever, Kerry proudly stood up for who and what she was.

'My mum really loves Bryan,' she confided. 'They get on really well. We live in a one-bedroom council flat and it's only small, so when Bryan stays she makes him sleep on the floor in the living room. I'm proud of where I live – even though we are buying a new house after Christmas. And then sometimes if I have to get up and go to work, he'll crawl into bed beside my mum – there's one for the gossip columns. I've met his family loads of times. At Christmas, I was really shocked because as well as his mum, his dad and his sister, there were loads of relatives and I had trouble trying to remember everyone's name. He's got such a big family and for us it's only me and Mum. Our family tree is a twig.' She clearly hadn't lost her sense of humour.

But work remained a big part of her life. Kerry's relationship with Bryan was all she had ever dreamed of – but then so was being a pop star. The band's third single, 'I Want Your Love', had given them their third Top Ten hit, not least down to a heavy TV marketing campaign and the fact that they acted as the main support act on the Steps tour. By October 2000, the band's schedule was as busy as ever, with that all-important first album on the way, and another single and tour coming up. 'We're doing the *Smash Hits* tour which is great,' crowed Kerry.

'That tour was where I first met Bryan, and Westlife are doing it, too, so it means I'll get to spend some time with him. Our début album *Right Now* is out on October 23 and tomorrow we've our new single "Follow Me" coming out. So far, we've had great reviews of the album, so we're very pleased. At the same time, we're really nervous as the better you do with your singles, the better you're known and the more pressure there is on you. But the album is fantastic – all the songs are great. My favourite is "Do What You Wanna", but they're all brilliant.' It was a revealing comment; the girls were also beginning to feel the pressures of success. When they started out, they had nothing to prove. Now, with three hits in the bag and their huge public profile, any faltering in their careers would be widely noted.

'Follow Me' was actually slightly different from the first three singles; it had an R 'n' B quality to it. The album, which included all four singles, also contained some diverse tracks, including their trademark energetic pop songs, as well as dance numbers and ballads. One of the ballads was 'Cradle', which had been featured in the film *Maybe Baby*. The marketing behind the music was as sharp as it had ever been and the girls were well aware of the pressure to continue to do well.

Kerry was becoming the consummate pop star, worrying about the balance of work and love life, but ever professional and ever willing to work as hard as she had to, to get the new record off the ground. She proved herself to be something of a good sport, too. The girls had turned up at an HMV shop in Scarborough, North Yorkshire, to sign records. When they got there, they were introduced to the shop's mascot, a Jack Russell called Nipper. Nipper took one look at Kerry and fell in love, an emotion he demonstrated by using her as a lamppost. The onlookers were agog.

'I don't think Kerry knew whether to laugh or cry at first – but the other band members thought it was hilarious,' said one. 'I think Nipper was overcome by all the attention the band was getting.' Kerry herself forgave him and carried on signing records – not something some divas, especially transatlantic ones, could be imagined doing under the circumstances, and the band's spokesman laughed it off. 'We tried not to let it put a damper on things,' he said. 'At least the occasion didn't go down the drain.'

But why not be good-humoured when everything else in her life was going so well? The relationship between Kerry and Bryan was now so serious that they decided to move in together, in a flat in London's Chelsea. 'It's really nice,' said Kerry, adding that she and Bryan were 'totally in love'. The pretence that they were just friends was now completely over; they were finally able to live as a proper couple. Indeed, Kerry was now revealing the full extent of the double life they had been leading, giggling as she recalled Atomic Kitten and Westlife turning up to the same events, where she and Bryan would have a furtive embrace and then carry on publicly as if they only knew each other as friends.

The girls were, by now, as much in demand as ever, not only commercially, but for charitable work, too. They were enlisted to support the Millennium Cup, a five-a-side football competition in aid of The Prince's Trust, with Kerry again keen to show other young people that a difficult childhood need not blight them for ever. Indeed, she was becoming something of a role model. 'I want to tell other kids who are going through what I went through that you can come out the other side and be someone,' she said. 'And that's what The Prince's Trust is all about – helping young people believe in themselves.'

It was around this time that Kerry and Bryan began to talk about marriage, and it might well have been now that Kerry first started to think about leaving Atomic Kitten. Life might have been exciting, but it was also frenetically highly paced, so much so that she was forced to take two weeks off citing nervous exhaustion. Coincidentally, Bryan did much the same thing over the summer. The pressures of the previous year had taken their toll; Kerry was the most high-profile of the Kittens and had gone from complete unknown to massive star almost overnight. It was hardly surprising that she was finding it difficult to cope, and she was prescribed anti-depressants.

'Kerry has been feeling down for a while,' said a sympathetic friend. 'A lot of it is down to the amount of work the girls have been doing promoting their new album. Some people who know Kerry well are also saying she's become disillusioned with the world of pop. It seems very exciting for a young girl at the outset with all the glitzy premières and parties but, in reality, it's one of the toughest jobs in the world.'

A spokesman for the band backed this up. 'I can confirm Kerry has been diagnosed with depression,' he said. 'She is having some time off to rest and get her energy levels back to normal. But we can assure fans the band will be back performing in the very near future.' With hindsight, of course, it should have been no surprise when, a couple of months on, Kerry did indeed decide to call it a day. But the members of Atomic Kitten had no option but to work as hard as they did. They knew that not only did they have to make an immediate impact – as, indeed, they had done – but that, in most cases, pop careers do not last that long and they had to take advantage of the opportunities while they were still being presented.

Meanwhile, after rumours suggesting that they were secretly engaged, Kerry and Bryan were also said to be under pressure from Westlife's record label, RCA, to keep the engagement a secret. 'RCA are desperately trying to keep it under wraps,' said a source. 'For a member of Britain's top boy band to become engaged is a disaster for them. After all, Westlife's biggest fans and those who buy the majority of their records are young girls. Bryan's posters are on the bedroom walls of teenage girls all over the country. So for them to find out he's getting married will be devastating for them.'

Indeed, the pressure had been on Bryan to keep the romance under wraps right from the start. And it was not only Kerry who wanted Atomic Kitten to succeed without being linked to Westlife. Westlife's manager, Louis Walsh, remained equally keen that all his boys should be seen to be available. But Kerry's presence in Bryan's life had become essential to him, and he talked openly about how his fiancée helped him overcome the depression he, too, had been experiencing. Indeed, given that both had been suffering from this darkest of ailments, they could quite clearly help and understand one another in a way that someone who has never experienced this condition could not.

'She is everything to me,' he said. 'Kerry's been my escape from the depression I have been feeling. To be honest, if it wasn't for her, I don't know where I would be now. She was there when I needed her the most and I have much to thank her for. When we were away for three months in America, things were at an all-time low for me. I missed home so much, I wanted to see my family again – especially my mum.

'Everything seemed dark – it's hard to explain. I was exhausted, mentally and physically. I couldn't see anything positive and the pressure was weighing down on me. I was smiling every night on stage, but inside I was at breaking point. I have learned a valuable lesson in the past few months. Money and fame can't make you happy. Two years ago, I would have said that they definitely could. But I'm not trying to get sympathy because I have a fantastic life now and I do know it. I am lucky to have the job that I do and the lifestyle that it brings. But I don't think the fans realise how tough a job it is. Then again, why should they? We are in this business to make them feel good, so there's no point in burdening them with our problems. But I wouldn't swap my place in Westlife for the world.'

These were not the whingings of a spoilt boy. Westlife – like Atomic Kitten – had an absolutely gruelling schedule and Bryan's account of the time his life was at its darkest, while on tour in America, is an illustration that being a pop star is not all fun and games. 'It happened when we were in

America this summer,' he said. 'It became a nightmare and that took its toll on me. We were up at five or six every morning for two-and-a-half months and it got to me and I physically couldn't take it. We were so tired that our work started to suffer. Once we flew in on an economy flight from Taiwan to Toronto. We then had a five-hour wait before flying to Detroit, where we were meant to connect to Ohio.

'The flight was cancelled and all the hotels were booked so we had to stay in a motel 20 miles away. We got there at 4.00am and it was disgusting. Two hours' sleep and then to New York and then Gatwick. I'd had two hours sleep in four days. The time I flipped was when we worked for 24 hours on our 'Against All Odds' single on the island of Capri. At 7.00am we got a ferry and flew to New York before doing a midnight show. When I came off stage later, I just collapsed. I was shaking in bed at 5.00am the next day and pulled open the mini-bar, ripping out all the bottles. I drank ten little bottles of vodka, scotch and gin, one after the other. I told the others, "I have to go home."'

It was a miracle, with all that work, that the relationship between the two had managed to blossom at all, let alone survive and thrive. And it is a very good explanation as to why so many people in the music industry end up either with a drink and drugs problem or go completely off the rails.

But Bryan and Kerry were ultimately professionals. If this

is what it took to be a pop star, then that is what they (or, at least, Bryan – Kerry was nearing the end of that stage of her career) would continue to do. Indeed, despite the angst, Bryan was well aware that Westlife owed everything to their fans, and revealed that he received thousands of fan letters every day. 'Some are really nice,' he said. 'A few are from girls who say they love you – even though they have never met you. I am very grateful for all our fans. You can't forget that they are the ones who put you there and can take the glory away in an instant.

'You have to be so aware that many of them look up to us – there's a lot of responsibility there. So it's not good enough just to put on a great stage show; you have to be part of the group even when you're enjoying yourself away from the band. If you get up to no good on a mad night out, then the chances are it's going to be in the papers the next day. So you have to be aware the fans see everything – you can't be hypocritical.' They were words that were going to come back to haunt him in the end.

But the two each clearly understood the pressures the other was under and continued to tell the world about their feelings for one another. Bryan even started talking about having children. 'I definitely want two – a girl and a boy – and I know what I'd call them already.' Of Kerry he said, 'Out of everything I have in my life, she makes me the happiest … We've been together now for a year but we've totally played it down. We wanted to keep it private, but we got photographed. I was seeing someone else when we first met and she was single. Then we started seeing loads of each other and I had to finish with the other girl. I just said to her, "Look, I'm in love with Kerry."

'I love surprising her. Like for her birthday – she had to go to Amsterdam to do *Top of the Pops*. I was supposed to go, too, but by the time I got there they wouldn't let me on the plane. She was devastated, crying and everything and it was the last flight. Luckily, there was a flight ten minutes later to Rotterdam. So I took that and then a taxi to Amsterdam. I knocked on her door at one o'clock in the morning and I'll never forget the look of surprise on her face.'

Rumours of an engagement continued, something that Bryan consistently denied. 'We speak to each other on the phone more than 30 times a day wherever we are in the world,' he revealed, although on another occasion he said it was actually five times a day, but the point was clear – they had to be constantly in touch. 'She is the first girl I've loved – my first proper girlfriend. This is the real thing and I can never see us splitting up. We are totally devoted to each other but we are not the new Posh and Becks. I can't get enough of Kerry. We aren't engaged although we have talked about marriage. I wear a friendship ring on my engagement finger but we wouldn't have time to get married, unless our record company gave me a day off.'

Whether or not they were talking about marriage, however, they were certainly making plans for the future. The couple decided to buy an 8,000 sq ft plot outside of

Dublin, on which to build a house where they could relax and enjoy their new found wealth. 'We're just waiting for the permission to come through so we can get started,' said a wildly excited Kerry. 'Hopefully it will be built by next Christmas. It will just be a nice house, bought with the money we've earned. A nice home for me and Bryan where, when we have finished work, we can go home and relax. It's just a tiny little village with one shop around the corner. My only disappointment is the pub is a bit too far away. We're going to have an indoor pool and everything. The full works. Why not? It's somewhere nice for Bryan and me to settle down and start a family in the future.' And if children were on the cards, then marriage was clearly an option, too.

Then Kerry indulged in that most modern of courtship rituals and had a new tattoo done, a picture of Winnie the Pooh transcribed on to her right buttock, next to Bryan's name. 'Pooh is my pet name for Bryan,' she confessed. And then, finally, it all came out – the couple were planning to marry in 2002 and, if the house was ready in time, they would do the ceremony there. 'It's gonna be a full-blown white wedding… the works,' said Kerry happily. 'It's every little girl's dream to grow up and have this great fairytale wedding. But I don't want to do it in a castle in Scotland like Madonna. I want a nice, proper wedding. I've got it all set out in my head. But if the new house is built, I'll do it at home and save us some money.'

They were also now ready to let on that they had, in fact,

been engaged for some time. 'The wheels were set in motion on Christmas Eve 1999,' confessed Bryan. 'I was on the phone to Kerry and we were besotted with each other. I told Kerry I definitely wanted to marry her. She said, "I want to marry you."'

Kerry added, 'So I flew over to Ireland on December 27,' she said, 'and the next day we drove to Donegal, which is about four hours from Dublin, and eventually pulled up outside Doe Castle. He took my hand and we climbed over this fence. He said, "Do you know why I've brought you here?" I said, "No." He said, "This is the spot where my grandad proposed to my nana." He then got down on his knees, pulled out a ring and asked me to marry him. I said, "Yes!" As soon as I could get to a phone, I called my mum to tell her – but she already knew. Bryan had phoned her beforehand to ask her if he could marry me, which I thought was very nice.'

Everyone was delighted for the couple; they were clearly utterly absorbed in one another and, in the couple of years leading up to the proposal, had had the same life experiences and so, again, could understand what the other was going through. There was, however, just one note of caution to be heeded – despite the fact that both were now old hands in the world of pop, both were actually still extremely young. Or to put it another way, both Kerry and Bryan were only twenty. Wasn't this a little early to start thinking about settling down?

Kerry was irritated by such talk. 'My mother was twenty

when she had me and Bryan's parents married when she was eighteen,' she said, 'so why should I be too young? We've been together just over a year now and there are definitely going to be many more years to come. I think it is really nice to show commitment to the world and that we are totally serious about each other. When we first started dating, everyone said it wasn't going to last. They gave it two weeks.'

Of course, with hindsight again, it is possible to see that Kerry was probably more mature than Bryan at this stage, and more able to take on all the responsibilities of married life. Her childhood had made her grow up quickly and, understandably, had given her a yearning to be settled. But that said, at the stage Bryan was just as keen as his bride-to-be to get married and have children. The bond between them was then very strong.

As if to make the point that this was the real thing, Kerry went to Dublin that year to spend Christmas with Bryan and his family, intending to visit her mother the following year. The traditional arrangement whereby a couple take it in turns to visit the in-laws, was under way. 'Kerry is coming to spend Christmas with me in Dublin,' said a jubilant Bryan. 'My parents think the world of her and it means a lot to me that she is coming over. We're just going to have a really nice, relaxing time together – we have to take advantage of every spare hour we get because normally we are away touring. It's going to be the best Christmas ever – I'm delighted that I can spend time with both my family and Kerry. I have already bought her a Christmas present – but I'm not going to tell anyone what it is yet. I've been planning this Christmas for a long time and I want everything to be perfect.'

They needed the break; the coming year was going to be tough. Westlife were due to spend at least five months touring the United States in a bid to make their breakthrough there, something they had still not managed, as well as at least two months on tour in Europe. Atomic Kitten was still riding high, and so Kerry was going to have to put in almost as much time touring as well. The pair would be parted for months at a time, which meant that the Christmas break was especially important.

'It's hard when you are away for months on end and we can't see each other,' said Bryan. 'I phone her at least five times a day – sometimes even more than that. By the end of the month, we have massive phone bills from all the time we have been talking to each other. Two weeks together at Christmas makes up for all the time we have spent apart. We're not going to be doing anything out of the ordinary over Christmas. We just want to relax and enjoy everything together before we have to get back to work again.

'I knew Kerry was the girl for me as soon as I met her. She is so full of life and so positive about things – I am so happy when I'm with her. We both decided to keep the relationship a secret at the start – even the rest of the guys in the band didn't know anything about it. The truth is that we had to. There was a lot of pressure on us to keep things quiet so we went along with it for a while. Thankfully, we don't have to keep things quiet any more – there's a bit more pressure from the media, but it's certainly worth it. After Christmas, we probably won't be able to see each other for another couple of months, so we want to make the most of this time together.'

And as far as Kerry was concerned, quite apart from spending time with Bryan, there was a lot to celebrate that Christmas. It had been an amazing, thrilling, tumultuous year. At the beginning of it she was just another pop wannabe and, at the end, she was a fully-fledged star in her own right. All the Kittens were famous, but Kerry in particular stood out. She was bright, brassy, cheerful, lively, sexy and very talkative. Now that her past was known about, she was widely respected for the way she had risen above difficult beginnings to make the world her own and, if all that was not enough, she was now engaged to one of the nation's heart-throbs. And on a personal level, she was soon going to be able to make her mother's life much more comfortable; the bond between Kerry and Sue was as strong as ever and this had been quite a year for Sue, too. She was utterly delighted by her daughter's success – and incredibly proud of the woman that Kerry had become.

5

KITTY LITTER

Fittingly, the Kittens finished 2000 on a high. The girls toured with Steps once again, in another sell-out tour. Everything they did, everywhere they went, made news. And then in December, they won not one but two prestigious awards – Best Newcomer at both the *Smash Hits* Poll Winner's Party and the Disney Awards. Their future in the world of pop seemed assured. They were ideally suited to it, too, being young, attractive and energetic. They were also perceived to have come from that most musical of cities, Liverpool, although Kerry, of course, actually came from nearby Warrington. But no matter … they looked and sounded the part.

After a short Christmas break, the Kittens reassembled, ready to take on the world once more. But something had changed. Kerry had found the year exhilarating but exhausting, had resented having to keep her relationship under wraps and was now at least as interested in a future as Mrs McFadden as she was in being an international pop star. And Kerry had a secret, a wonderful secret which she was about to share with the rest of the world. She was going to have a baby. Motherhood was something she had always aspired to; now, scarcely out of her teens, it was finally going to happen.

And so she made a decision which left the world of showbusiness in shock. Kerry Katona, arguably the bubbliest of three bubbly girls, was leaving Atomic Kitten. The girls had had a sensational year and really did seem to be on the verge of superstar status. How on earth could she even consider leaving the band? But Kerry was adamant. For all its successes, 2000 had been an exhausting year both for her and for Bryan and, now that she was expecting his baby, she wanted to leave. She had everything she'd ever hoped for and she quite genuinely saw no reason not to leave the Atomic Kitten. It had almost been by chance that she'd become a pop star, after all, and she reasoned that now she had a profile she could put it to good use elsewhere.

But Kerry was not the only one to be affected by her decision and so some very quick thinking went on behind the scenes. Atomic Kitten quite clearly still had a big future ahead of them, and so there was no question of breaking up the rest of the group. Instead, they turned to Jenny Frost, whom the girls all knew well. Until then a singer with the girl band Precious, Jenny had quite frequently bumped into

Atomic Kitten on shows and tours in the past; now that Kerry was leaving, she was the perfect choice.

And so, the decision taken, the mantle was handed from Kerry to Jenny and Kerry stepped down from the band. She had no regrets about leaving but, still, it was the end of an era. 'I will miss the girls so much,' she said. 'I have had such a fantastic time in Atomic Kitten over the last year. At the moment, I just want to be a mum and I don't want to work at the same time because I need complete rest for a healthy baby. I think leaving Atomic Kitten is the most sensible thing to do; I'm going to sit at home, watch TV, eat chocolate and take it one day at a time.

'I've had a good cry with Liz and Tash and they are so supportive. We talk all the time and I just know we'll always be really close. I think it's great that Jenny is joining. I've known her for ages and she's very funny, she's just like the other girls. I'm devastated at going but I'm thrilled for Jenny, she's a great pal and I know she'll make a great kitten.'

Those were typically generous words from Kerry; she really was delighted for her friend. But she was looking forward to the future, too. Kerry was not merely expecting a baby; she was utterly exhausted over a year of hard work and she badly needed a rest.

As for Atomic Kitten's management, they could not have been kinder and more gracious to the soon-to-be-ex-Kitten. Kerry's desire to leave might have caused a few problems, but they saw at first hand exactly what being a member of the group involved, and so understood Kerry's decision. 'We can confirm that Kerry Katona is leaving Atomic Kitten after she completes promotion for the band's current single, "Whole Again",' said the band's manager Stuart Bell. 'Since she decided to leave the band, Kerry has worked closely with myself, Liz and Natasha to find the right person to replace her – a tall order, we know – but we do feel we have found a true star in Jenny.

'The Kitten's team is a very close-knit family and we were all thrilled with the news of Kerry's pregnancy and completely understand her decision to put the wellbeing of her unborn child first. Being in Atomic Kitten is a 24-hour-a-day, hectic way of life, which really wouldn't make for a stress-free, relaxed pregnancy. All of us at Integral, Engine and Innocent Records want to take this opportunity to wish Kerry and Bryan the best for their baby and their forthcoming marriage.'

The wisdom of her decision became plain almost at once. Kerry had planned to stay on into February to help launch the new single but, in the event, she ended up leaving earlier than expected. After becoming quite stressed, her doctors advised complete rest and so she left before the promotion schedule was complete and watched what happened to the band from the sidelines.

As it happens, Kerry just missed out on the group's first Number One; shortly after her departure, 'Whole Again' was released on 29 January 2001 and went straight to the top of the charts, beating U2 for the prime spot. But Kerry was quite genuinely unconcerned. She could not wait for motherhood; the baby was due in September, one day before her 21st birthday, and she and Bryan had already revealed that if it was a girl she would be called Molly and, if a boy, DJ, short for Dylan James. Indeed, they had discussed the names even before Kerry had got pregnant, such was their desire to start a family together. 'I just can't wait to get dead fat and lie around,' said Kerry. 'There'll be no drinks or showbiz parties for me for a while. I couldn't be happier, my family are ecstatic and Lil and Tash can't wait to get down to Baby Gap.'

The pregnancy was not planned; when talking about it in early January, Bryan said that he was shocked, but very happy. Indeed, they both were. 'I worked out that I must have got pregnant in the Conrad [Hotel] the night before we shot the video for our new single "Whole Again",' said Kerry. 'But that was only after Bryan convinced me to take a pregnancy test some weeks later. I thought I was stressed because I was tired, then Bryan said I should do a pregnancy test. When the test was positive, I was so stunned I wet myself, then I started laughing hysterically. As soon as Bryan and I got our heads round the idea, we were over the moon.'

Bryan was, indeed, utterly delighted at the idea of becoming a father. The couple were engaged, after all; why wait now before starting a family proper? He was also completely supportive of Kerry's decision to quit the group – and she was not abandoning showbusiness completely, for she had already revealed that she would now like to pursue a career as a television presenter. But for the present, there was just to be quiet and rest.

'I can't wait to be a mum and have a family with Bryan,' she said. 'I told him I wanted a completely stress-free pregnancy. That's why I decided to leave the band and Bryan backed me all the way. I could have stayed in the band if I'd wanted, but I didn't really fancy prancing around on stage with a great big belly hanging out. I'd much rather be a mum than a pop star. But I'm still thrilled the record got to Number One because, of course, it's my voice on the record.

'I still talk to the girls every day because we're like sisters. And I'm going out to celebrate with them on Thursday. I'm not such a party animal as I was before but I think I'll let myself have one glass of wine – because that's allowed – but I'll make sure it's a big glass. Then I'm back on the water and I get so tired that I'll probably only last 'til about 11.00pm. Some party! But I wouldn't miss it.'

Of course, Kerry was pleased about the single – after all, it was recorded while she was still in the band – but motherhood was something else again. It was something Kerry had always wanted. She once confessed that before she became a pop star, she'd wanted to be a nanny, and that both she and Bryan adored children. Bryan was also clear that Kerry was made for the role. 'Kerry's going to be a brilliant mum,' he once said, before they discovered she was pregnant. 'Because she grew up with so many foster parents and stuff, and because she didn't have a proper childhood, she wants to make sure her kids have the best life possible.'

Kerry, however, was discovering, as so many women do, that her pregnancy was not plain sailing. She was still only two months' pregnant when she first made the announcement that she was going to have a baby and leave the band, and was therefore wildly emotional at this early stage. 'I've been a right cow to Bryan recently – my hormones have been all over the place,' she said. 'One minute I'm happy, the next I'm sobbing my eyes out or I'm in a foul mood. I've really been taking it out on Bryan, but he's so sweet I couldn't ask for a better boyfriend.'

As for her age, Kerry remained indignant if anyone suggested that she was very young for motherhood. 'The baby is due on September 5, the day before my 21st birthday,' she said. 'I don't believe I'm too young to be a mother. I'm a woman, not a child. I know how to look after myself and I know I will be able to look after a baby. My mum Sue lives in a one-bedroom council flat in Warrington and that's where I stay when I go back home.

'She'll be moving soon, into the new three-bedroom house I bought her at Christmas. But she'll stay with me in the new house Bryan and I have bought in Ireland while I have the baby. Mum and me are really close. When I told her I was pregnant, she was so happy she started crying. She never once asked me if I wanted to keep the baby. I'm sure being without the girls will feel strange, but it will also be a relief to put all the travelling and showbiz parties behind me. I want to have the same close relationship with my baby that I have with my mum. I'm looking forward to getting fat and lying about in my pyjamas watching black-and-white movies, then making a home with Bryan and showering my child with love.'

And, true to her word, Kerry did adopt a lower profile until her baby was born. She retreated to Ireland, initially planning to live in a house she and Bryan had bought in Delgany, County Wicklow. However, her aim for a quiet life did not go according to plan due to the attentions of local youths jealous of the couple's wealth and success. Malicious behaviour driven by envy is a problem any famous person has to put up with but Kerry had a particularly unpleasant couple of experiences – and this after having left the band that had made her name.

The first incident, which would have been terrifying for anyone, but particularly for a pregnant woman, came about when Kerry accompanied Bryan to a football match in the evening at Tallaght, Dublin. He got out of the car to join his Aer Lingus team-mates, whereupon Kerry locked the doors and settled down with a magazine.

What happened next was shameful. When a group of hooligans recognised who was sitting in the BMW, they surrounded it and first began to pelt it with stones. Then they began rocking it from side to side, while one of the gang mooned at poor Kerry. Unsurprisingly, she was screaming by this point and, finally, Bryan and the team realised what was going on and chased the offenders away.

'I feared for my life and for the baby's too,' said a shocked Kerry. 'I didn't know what to do. I kept thinking the car would roll over.' She was badly shaken by the experience, although, thankfully, both she and the baby were ultimately unharmed.

The next problem surfaced in the form of the topless pictures, which were thrust yet again into the public domain. This time the magazine *Private Lives* had got hold of them and was preparing to publish. Kerry, who by now must have been rueing the day she went to that photographer only a few short years ago, had to go to the High Court to get them banned.

If that was not enough, the next blow was the biggest of all. The couple's house in Delgany was perfect for a new family; set in a quarter-of-an-acre, with spectacular views over the surrounding countryside, it had five bedrooms and a huge conservatory. But some locals destroyed that particular dream before it had even started, in yet another example of the envy fame can cause. Kerry and Bryan began receiving hate mail and personal abuse in the streets when they visited the house. They were forced to sell it before they'd even moved in.

Matters began to improve, however, in July. For a start, the couple discovered that Kerry was expecting a girl, something that thrilled both of them. 'I am so excited about being a dad and when I found out we were expecting a girl, I was so happy,' said Bryan. 'But to be honest, it didn't matter to either of us what sex the baby was, as long as it was healthy. When they told us, we just hugged and kissed each other. It was very emotional. We were already over the moon at Kerry being pregnant. But now we know the sex we just can't wait for her to be born.

'But I do feel sorry for the boyfriends who come round when Molly is fifteen or sixteen as I will give them a pretty hard time! No, seriously, we will always support her in anything she wants to do.' And he, too, felt it was something to celebrate after the recent problems. 'It's been a rough few months to say the least, but hopefully that's all in the past and we can get on with our lives again,' he said. 'It was just horrible.'

The rest of the summer passed quietly. There was intensive speculation as to when and where the wedding would be taking place, with almost every castle in the whole of Britain and Ireland getting a mention at some point in the press, but Kerry and Bryan were not yet ready to reveal their plans. They were also getting ready for the new arrival, painting *Jungle Book* characters on the wall of the nursery. Life was becoming extremely happy once more.

And the two of them remained besotted with each other. Bryan spoke many times about his feelings for Kerry, once saying, 'Her generosity is one of the qualities I admire her so much for. I used to think so many girls were beautiful – until I went out with Kerry, and now every woman pales in comparison. There's something in her eyes, just something about her. In my eyes, she's pure perfection.

'And, of course, she's one of the lads. She'll come out

with the five of us from Westlife and just fit in like a boy. She's got three personas – her stage persona, her tomboy persona and her dead posh persona when she talks to my mum.' This was typical of the way that Bryan spoke about Kerry; he could not sing her praises highly enough. He talked about her constantly, wrote songs for her and credited her with bringing everything that was good into his life. Kerry was equally head over heels in love with him; they could not have been happier prospective parents.

Molly Marie McFadden finally arrived on 31 August 2001, a few days early, weighing in at 8lb 2oz. She was born in Dublin's Mount Carmel Hospital, with her father Bryan and her grandmother Sue at her mother's side. It was a difficult labour, lasting for about 18 hours, but the proud parents could barely contain their joy. 'We are going to spoil her rotten and I am not ashamed to say that,' said a highly emotional Kerry. 'She is the best thing that has ever happened to myself and Bryan – better than any hit record. I want to give her the security I never had as a child.'

Bryan, who emerged from the hospital the day after his daughter's birth with a sleeping bag under his arm, was equally besotted with the new arrival. 'They were terrified something was going to go wrong,' said a friend of the couple. 'But everything went fine and they are all just exhausted now. Bryan just won't stop looking at Molly and holding her hand. He's already playing the role of the protective father.' And his colleagues in Westlife also sent in their support. 'We all feel like uncles to Molly and we would like to welcome her as the newest member of Westlife,' they said.

Indeed, Bryan seemed quite overwhelmed by his new role as a father. 'It's one of the greatest feelings I've ever had in my life,' he said. 'I've always wanted to have children, but I didn't think I'd be a father so soon. You only realise what it's all about when the baby finally arrives. All I was worried about was that the baby would be healthy, whichever sex it would be. Now I am just so proud that Molly is not only a healthy baby but also very, very beautiful. I could not be happier.

'Myself and Kerry feel so lucky. I broke down and cried when Molly finally arrived and I held her little body in my arms. She has Kerry's blonde hair and she's already shown she has a great pair of lungs. I'm taking a few weeks off to help now. I don't want to do anything other than be around Kerry and Molly.' Proud father barely sums it up – Bryan was on cloud nine.

Indeed, so happy was he that he went out that weekend and indulged in a sing-song almost entirely devoted to the couple's new baby. He went to Lillie's Bordello that Saturday night and, with Moby from U2 on the piano, he sang a range of traditional Irish melodies, including 'My Irish Molly' and 'Molly Malone'.

Accompanying him were the footballer Robbie Keane and the broadcaster Eamon Dunphy. And he was as good as his word, taking a month off from performing with Westlife, before reuniting with them at the Disney

Channel Kids Awards in London. Fatherhood was clearly taking its toll. 'I've had hardly any sleep since Molly was born – I get about three hours a night now,' he said. 'But it's all worth it.'

And now that Molly had actually been born, Kerry and Bryan were able to start planning their wedding. It had been erroneously reported that the two were to marry in the summer of the following year; now it emerged that the actual wedding date was to be 5 January 2002 and the marriage was to take place at Slane Castle, Meath, in Ireland.

Bryan, of course, now had to return to work on a more permanent basis. Given that he was still the member of a band, he could not stay away indefinitely and, at some point, was going to have to rejoin the rest of Westlife on the road, which meant that he was going to be separated not just from Kerry, but from Molly, too.

Indeed, Westlife were beginning to plan their next world tour, which meant being away for some time. Bryan clearly had very mixed feelings about the prospect. 'I think it is something I am going to have to deal with when it comes along,' he said. 'It has already been difficult being away from her since she was born and, obviously, the tour will be tough in that respect, but I am looking forward to it all the same.' He also continued to feel self-conscious about some aspects of being in the band. 'I don't like going into a shop and having people looking at me,' he said. 'It's not a big-headed thing but I really don't like it. Sometimes, I feel I am part of a freak show. I feel I have two heads.'

The problem was soon resolved; Kerry and Molly would come with him on tour. Bryan continued to talk about how happy Molly made him. 'It has been just brilliant. It has made me,' he said. 'And it has worked really well with the rest of the band – it feels like we are more of a family now. The others look on Molly, who is now two months, like they are her uncles. They feel responsible for her. Molly and Kerry will come on tour with me so it will not have any impact on Westlife and I'm happier than I have ever been.'

It was really quite touching to hear Bryan talking about his daughter. Many men are quite overwhelmed when they first experience fatherhood proper and Bryan was clearly one of their number; he was also conceding that his priorities had changed completely. 'Before Molly, I didn't like Westlife,' he said. 'I felt tired and didn't want to be in it any more – although I never talked about it. The fun had gone out of it. It wasn't interesting or exciting. I had a lot of money, but I didn't really care. I wasn't spending money on important things, I was spending it on crap. When Molly came along, my approach changed. I was buying nappies and clothes and I realised you have a certain amount to spend each week. Money starts to matter. Before, it was, "If I make a million, I'll buy a Ferrari." Now, if I make a million, I can look after Molly for a while.'

Indeed, Bryan was so swept away by his baby that he couldn't help thinking about the impact she made on other people, too. 'The baby brought it into perspective for everyone,' he said. 'It has made them think the way I am thinking, that it isn't going to last for ever. They are now taking life more seriously.' As for his feelings about Kerry, Molly's arrival only increased his devotion. 'It was amazing how quickly Kerry became the ultimate mother,' he said. 'I love her a lot more now. I have always loved her to bits, but now I love her in a different way. She's the mother of my child. Now we are a family.'

It was quite a change, to have gone from a member of a boy band who was not even allowed to admit he had a girlfriend to doting father about to get married, but Bryan made the leap with aplomb. 'It's not that I don't care what the fans think, but I don't think the fans actually care,' he said. 'Maybe if it was Shane or Nicky it would be different, but I don't think I have ever been seen as the hunk. I am the one people want to have a laugh with in the pub. People were happy for me. I've had no bad feedback.'

As for the fact that he and Kerry were still extremely young, like his wife-to-be, Bryan was adamant that there was no problem. 'I am having a baby at the perfect age,' he said. 'When I am 42, Molly will be 21 and me and Kerry will still be young enough to have our own life. We definitely see ourselves together in 50 years. I definitely want to die with Kerry. Kian said to me recently, "You are the richest man in the world." And I definitely am. You could take all the money away and I would still be the richest man in the world.'

Indeed, both parents were so enamoured of their child

that they were already thinking about having another one. 'Having Molly has made me really broody,' she said. 'We want to have another one next year. Molly's just so beautiful, I've never been happier. She's got my eyes but Bryan's nose and mouth. Bryan is just brilliant with her. He dotes on her so much, we both do.'

Kerry was also ready to resume her career, albeit a slightly different one from her former life as a pop star. After leaving Atomic Kitten, she had announced plans to work as a television presenter and, in October 2001, she found the first opportunity to do so. Richard and Judy had recently left *This Morning* and Kerry and Bryan stepped into the breach for three days with John Leslie and Coleen Nolan. The two acted as pop interviewers to the likes of S Club 7, Steps and Mis-Teeq.

'I am really proud to be presenting such a high-profile show,' said Kerry and, indeed, it was a perfect transition from the world of pop to that of television. 'They did very well and seemed to really enjoy themselves, but I think they found it harder than they thought,' said a spokesman for the show. It went well enough, though, for her to set up meetings with more executives in the television industry; her ambition to become a television presenter looked as if it was going to come true.

The couple were becoming more settled; they'd bought a flat in the middle of Dublin and found that was far more to their taste than living in the country. Kerry had had enough of life on the road as a pop star, but she did intend to continue her career in showbusiness. She put in an appearance at December's *Smash Hits* award show, while Bryan once again paid tribute to all that she had done for him. 'Without her coming into my life, Westlife wouldn't be here as it is today,' he said.

The problem was still the band's utterly exhausting schedule. 'It was changing me,' Bryan said. 'We had been travelling so much and doing endless promotion and all the spirit in me was being sucked out. I wasn't happy any more. If Kerry hadn't come into my life, I would have been on drugs by now. I was so unhappy that I would probably have needed something like that. Kerry put my feet back on the ground and brought back all the happiness. I'm high on life again because she is there with me.' He was clearly doting on his fiancée.

Of course, Kerry was equally happy; with a beautiful new baby and a promising start to a career in television, the year was again ending on a high note. She was settled in Ireland now, the couple were already thinking about having another baby and she was, after all, still only twenty-one. She had something else on her mind, too. She had a wedding to plan.

6

A PERFECT WEDDING

If truth be told, the preparations had been going on for months. The couple had, after all, been engaged for nearly two years, but were leaving nothing to chance; they engaged the services of two wedding planners to coordinate what was already being described as the showbusiness wedding of the year. And both were getting increasingly excited as the big day approached. Their celebrity – especially their joint celebrity – was now such that a huge amount of interest was already being shown in the nuptials, with intensive speculation about the time, the place… and, of course, what the bride would choose to wear on the big day.

But the couple were busy making plans. 'There is just so much to do, so much to organise because we want it to be extra special,' said Bryan, two months before the wedding was due to take place. 'Kerry will have five bridesmaids and Natasha Hamilton from Atomic Kitten will be one of them. Shane is the only member of the band to be one of my groomsmen as we are the closest in the group. My friend Eddie is going to be my Best Man. I can't tell you much more about it but it will have a very Christmassy feel.'

One of the reasons Bryan couldn't talk too freely, of course, was because the couple had signed a deal with *Hello!* magazine to cover the nuptials. And secrecy was the name of the game. The address of the wedding was not actually on the invitations that had been sent out; instead, guests were to be collected by limousines and taken on to the location, although it was quite widely known that the reception was to be held at Slane Castle.

It was a sensible decision. Kerry and Bryan, and many other celebrities, have often been criticised for cashing in, as others see it, on their wedding and taking a big cash payment in return for coverage of the big day. In actual fact, it is one of the best ways of ensuring a wedding goes according to plan. Very famous people, as Kerry and Bryan now were, were simply not able to marry in their local church and hold a private reception for family and friends. The fans coming to watch the proceedings and would-be gate crashers put a stop to that. In order to avoid this, many opt for the celebrity magazine route, not just to defray the cost of the proceedings (which, in this case, as many others, turned out to be substantial), but to put the arrangements in the hands of an organisation that has a vested interest in keeping the proceedings under wraps.

And as much as a showbusiness wedding of the year could, the marriage of Kerry and Bryan was to retain the flavour of a family affair. Eddie, Bryan's Best Man, was Eddie Loughlin, a friend of the singer since childhood and it was significant Bryan chose him rather than another famous friend. Both Kerry and Bryan were keen to invite not only their current celebrity friends to the wedding, but also people they had known from before they were famous. 'Eddie has been Bryan's best mate for years and they've stuck together through thick and thin,' said a friend. 'He was delighted when Bryan asked him to be Best Man. They have been hanging around together since they were toddlers.'

Of course, Kerry had nothing like as many childhood friends as Bryan, but members of her family were also to play a prominent role on the day.

Kerry and Bryan were also taking a conventional approach to the forthcoming nuptials, deciding, as tradition dictates, to spend the night before the wedding apart. Bryan determined to go and spend the night at his mother's, while Sue, utterly thrilled for her daughter, went to stay with Kerry and Molly at their home in Dublin. 'Bryan is very superstitious and doesn't want to see Kerry, as it is meant to be bad luck,' said a friend. 'They will see each other for a while on Friday afternoon and then Bryan will go back to his old home where he grew up. He's going to go out with

Dane Bowers and his friends for a few pints on Friday night just to relax him. The rest of the Westlife lads will be with him, too, so it should be a good celebration as his last night as a single man. He is very nervous but they both can't wait. It's going to be the showbiz wedding of the year.' Of course, this also gave both sets of families the chance for confidence-boosting and mutual support just before the ceremony was due to take place.

There had been some speculation that Westlife would perform at the wedding, but it was decided that the boys should be allowed to relax and enjoy themselves instead. Their schedule had been extremely onerous in recent months and this was not just seen as Bryan's big day for him alone, but for the rest of them to have an opportunity to relax as well. 'They aren't going to perform because they want to enjoy the celebrations,' said an insider. 'Initially, there was a plan for the lads to sing a collection of their hits at the start of the meal at Slane Castle.

'But now they just want to enjoy the day with Bryan and party like everyone else. They'll have a few glasses of champagne and get into the party mood. They have been working extremely hard and deserve a good night out. But there's every chance that they could get up on stage later in the night and have a sing-song on the spur of the moment.'

Instead, the official entertainment was to be provided by Paul Harrington, who, in 1994, had won the Eurovision Song Contest with the song 'Rock and Roll Kids' and who remained a massively popular entertainer. 'Paul is the perfect choice because he can turn his hand to any song,' said one of the people involved in organising the proceedings. 'He's been a big star in Ireland since winning the contest and Bryan and Kerry thought he was the perfect choice to provide the music. Dane Bowers will also be spinning a few tunes for some of the younger guests.' The billing as showbiz wedding of the year was beginning to look particularly apt.

Kerry was also getting thoroughly excited as the big day approached. All her life, she had dreamed of a big, white wedding; now that fantasy was finally going to turn into a reality, and she could scarcely believe it was happening to her. Not that it stopped her from viewing the proceedings in a typically Kerry-like way. 'It's definitely a dream come true for me,' she said. 'I'm going to be totally outnumbered at the church. There are only about 20 people in my family and Bryan has hundreds. He has so many cousins and around 200 of the guests are people related to him. Normally at a wedding, there's one side for the bride's guests and one for the groom's. But at ours, Bryan's guests are going to spill right over and take up nearly the entire church.'

The church where the wedding was to take place was the Church of the Immaculate Conception in the tiny village of Rathfeigh. The couple were going to be married in style.

As news spread of the forthcoming nuptials, even the locals were looking forward to the big day. Indeed, many were thrilled to know that the glitz and glamour of showbusiness was reaching their particular corner of Ireland. 'None of us had any idea until we read it in the *Irish Mirror* the other day,' said James Mawhinney, who lived nearby. 'We all know the church but we hadn't even heard a whisper that Bryan and Kerry are getting married there. My kids are both big Westlife fans and would never have forgiven me if they had come and gone without them knowing. I'll definitely be taking the kids down to see what is going on.'

Another local, Breda Lee, agreed. 'It's going to be a very exciting day – nothing like this village has ever experienced before,' she said. 'We had no idea that there was going to be such a big wedding here until we read it in the paper. It's the perfect location and the church is so beautiful. I'll be taking my kids down to have a look at it all. I'm a massive Westlife fan, as are my kids.'

One of the wedding planners was Tara Fay, one of Ireland's top experts in the field. Also involved in the organisation was the PR supremo Joanne Byrne. Between the two of them, they were planning a spectacular event; if anything, it was almost taking on the characteristics of a medieval feast, with a sumptuous repast, music – of course – magicians and revelry. In the best showbiz traditions, the bride and groom would sport not one outfit, but two; their guests would also be dressed in the most fashionable and glamorous outfits.

In their happiness, the bride and groom wanted to be generous, telling friends and family that they didn't want wedding presents and they should make a donation to charity instead. After all, they had been a couple for two years, and had lived together through much of that time, accumulating all they needed for their household. Kerry had certainly not forgotten her roots – she hasn't done to this day – but she had been living in much less impoverished circumstances than she had done as a child, and so there was nothing material she felt she needed.

The couple were also planning a brief honeymoon. 'It's going to be somewhere hot,' confided Bryan. 'But we don't want to say exactly where it is and get photographers following us over there. Because of Westlife, we can't go away for two weeks, but we'll get away for a week and make the most of it.' Of course, when they did manage to get away, they were spotted almost immediately – but coped with the interest the public was showing in them remarkably well.

On the big day itself, nothing was left to chance. For a start, there was a heavy police presence, with about a dozen members of the Gardai actually at the church and about thirty more in the area. This was necessary. Both Kerry and Bryan had had problems with difficult fans in the past and neither wanted this day, of all days, to end in trouble. 'It is our duty to anticipate and control danger,' said a Gardai spokesman, queried about the number of officers present. 'This was responsible management on our part. Bryan McFadden's promotional people would have alerted us to the fact that this wedding was going ahead. And with large crowds expected, we had to take safety precautions, especially where young children are concerned.' There was some criticism in the press about the numbers of officers present, but it was unjustified. There were a large number of stars present on the day and concerns about safety were real.

Bride and groom were both a little tense after all the build-up to the big day, but were determined to maintain an aura of tranquillity. Bryan spent the morning in the grounds of Slane Castle, calming his nerves by racing around on a quad bike and indulging in a spot of clay pigeon shooting. He was accompanied by Kian Egan. 'Kian's a lot better on the bikes than I am so I had difficulty keeping up with him,' Bryan said. 'I was also conscious that I didn't want to hurt myself on the big day of my wedding. But the grounds around the castle are quite lush and spacious, so it's ideal for whizzing around on bikes.' It was also ideal for working off all that excess energy. As the day wore on, a palpable excitement was to be felt in the air.

About 100 fans turned up to see the wedding but, because of the magazine deal, were not able to see the bride and groom. Their security people held up black screens to allow them to get into the church without being spotted by the public, something that aroused some negative comment from bystanders, but which did nothing to spoil the day. Bryan and his Best Man Eddie arrived for the 3.00pm ceremony first; they appeared in a black Mercedes, and were escorted through the police cordon by two police motorcyclists.

Kerry, as is the bride's privilege, was an hour late; she was driven up to the church in a sleek Rolls-Royce and slipped inside behind the screens, as did her chief bridesmaid, Natasha Hamilton. Later, she good-naturedly pointed the finger of blame elsewhere. 'Nobody realises it was actually my aunt who held up the whole wedding,' she said. 'She arrived really late and the bridesmaids were also with her, so that's why I ended up coming to the church an hour after everyone else had arrived.'

Not all of the 250 guests were so coy when it came to concealing themselves, which afforded some opportunities for star spotting from the gathered crowd. Bryan's Westlife band member Nicky Byrne was one of the first guests to arrive at the church with his fiancée Georgina, the daughter of Irish Taoiseach Bertie Ahern, in the perfect fusion of pop and politics. Indeed, Westlife, of course, were lending their full support – Kian, Shane Filan and Mark Feehily were there, as was their manager Louis Walsh.

To the great thrill of the crowds, Ronan Keating and his wife Yvonne were also in attendance, as was Bryan Kennedy and that other Atomic Kitten, Liz McClarnon. Brian Kennedy was another guest, along with UTV presenter Gerry Kelly, Freddie Middleton, the chief executive of BMG records and Lord Henry Mountcharles, the owner of Slane Castle. In other words, it was one of the starriest gatherings to be held in Ireland that year, with some of the country's most important and influential showbiz figures present.

And then, of course, there was Bryan's family. Kerry was still a bit bemused by the size of the clan she was marrying into. 'I was an only child and I didn't know my dad, so I'd like to have a big family,' she explained afterwards. 'Bryan's from a big family. His mum's one of eleven and his dad's one of fifteen. The wedding was just ridiculous, with all the cousins and that. People came over to me and said, "Hi, I'm Bryan's aunt," and "I'm Bryan's second aunt," and "I'm Bryan's third cousin." One said, "Hi, you met me, remember?" And I said, "I'm not being funny, but there are so many of you I don't have a clue! You're all going to have to get name tags!"'

Inside, the church had been beautifully decorated with roses and lilies by the Dublin-based florist James Bailie, who had also done Slane Castle for the reception later on in the day. The display was spectacular; there were gasps from the guests as they went inside. The ceremony itself was conducted by Father Joe Gleeson, the local priest, and Father JJ Mullen, who had been chaplain when Bryan was at school. And now that she had entered the church, the guests could finally see the bride in all her splendour. Kerry was wearing a beautiful, long cream strapless dress, which cost around £10,000, comprising a duchesse satin basque and skirt designed by Neil Cunningham, with a diamond tiara and long veil to set it off. Her beloved foster-father, Fred Woodhall, was there to give her away, while her Aunt Angela was acting as Maid of Honour. Her mother was beaming, quite overcome with pride, from the pews.

Bryan was wearing a gold frock coat and burgundy-and-gold waistcoat by Louis Copeland, while the respective mothers, Sue and Mairead, were both wearing outfits by the Irish designer Deborah Veale – a graceful gesture by Sue towards the country that Kerry now intended to make her home. Baby Molly was also present, gurgling away, although there were also a few tears during the service. 'She looked so cute, smiling away,' Bryan said afterwards. 'She's a dream baby.'

The ceremony was a typical Irish Catholic wedding, but there were a couple of points that stood out. For a start, Bryan, nervous as he was, managed to make a joke. In Irish weddings it is traditional for the bride to be given something gold and something silver; when the moment came for Kerry to receive her gifts, Bryan quipped to the congregation, 'Has anyone got any euros?' It got quite a laugh from everyone present.

Second, and rather more memorably, Bryan and Kerry got a telegram from the late Pope John Paul II. Bryan had actually met the Pope the previous month when Westlife had performed on a Christmas TV Show at the Vatican. The Pontiff had remembered the nuptials and sent a message saying, 'Bless you, Brian, and bless you, Kerry, on your wedding day.' Again, the contrast between Kerry's childhood and her life now as an adult could not have been more acute. Not only was she getting married in a splendid ceremony, but she had even received a personal blessing from the Pope.

And there were plenty of other features that made the wedding stand out, too. Indeed, it might have been an Irish Catholic service, but the ceremony was also in the best showbusiness tradition. With so many singers present, how could the music not have been spectacular? Hymns were sung by the RTE choir, a black gospel choir, and Dane Bowers sang the song 'From the Heart', a song with a particular meaning for Bryan and Kerry. 'Dane's is a song that's very special to Kerry and me, so to have that song for our wedding, sung live by Dane, was really special,' Bryan explained. The couple exchanged diamond-encrusted platinum rings, in a ceremony that was quite as beautiful and touching as anyone could have wished.

When the official events at the church were over, it was time to move on to the reception, where the guests felt that the solemn aspect of the occasion had been dealt with and that they could now let their hair down. Slane Castle was nine miles away and the bride and groom were escorted under cover again to the party, where the real festivities got under way. And it was all quite spectacular; the castle had been decorated as beautifully as the church. Neither was the grandeur of the surroundings lost on the bride and groom themselves – both could scarcely believe where they were. 'I used to come to pop concerts in the grounds of Slane and look up at the castle,' said Bryan. 'But I never, ever imagined in a million years that I'd be getting married there.'

Dinner was sumptuous – melon and vegetable soup,

followed by Irish beef and sticky toffee pudding with butterscotch sauce and fresh fruit. Guests were given a coin as a momento of the big day, with a euro insignia on one side and Kerry and Bryan inscribed on the other. 'The coins are not legal tender or anything, they are just a momento,' said one guest. 'Bryan and Kerry thought it would be nice to give guests something to remember the big day.' They would have been hard pressed not to. The wedding and the reception had turned out to be everything Kerry and Bryan had hoped for; it truly was one of the showbiz events of the year.

The mood could not have been happier or more celebratory. Everyone, it seemed, made speeches. Both the bride and groom stood up to have their say, as did Fred Woodhall, Eddie Loughlin and the groomsmen. The atmosphere could not have been more joyous; everyone was delighted for the happy couple, both of whom looked utterly joyful throughout. It was the wedding Kerry had always wanted.

And so to the dancing. After the speeches, Kerry slipped away and put on a slinky black number that was identical, in all but colour, to her wedding dress. It was quite stunning. 'When the black dress arrived, a couple of days before the wedding, I wanted to get married in it instead,' she said. Bryan, meanwhile, put on a white tie and tails to lead his new wife to the dance floor for the first dance of their married life. The song they chose was Dr Hook's 'Years from Now'. 'We both wanted to make our first dance really special and, looking back at the pictures, it was a great moment,' said Bryan.

With so many singers present, it was inevitable that some, not least among them Bryan, would take to the mike. Indeed, Bryan very nearly put on a mini-concert, singing, among others, '(I Can't Get No) Satisfaction' and 'We Are Family', much to the great enjoyment of the guests. Blues singer Lee Ryan then sang 'I Want You Back', after which Ronan gave a rendition of 'When You Say Nothing At All'. Some of the performances were in public and some in the bedrooms, as the guests began to spread out within the castle. Westlife themselves put on a performance, while Paul Harrington, the official entertainer, wowed the guests with his repertoire. As with everything else, the entertainment was judged to be perfect.

Meanwhile, to make the night even more memorable, a magician put on a virtuoso display for the guests. The spectacle then got even better; a massive firework display outside the castle followed, with the words 'Bryan Loves Kerry' spelt out, followed by the name Molly. The festivities went on well into the night, until the happy couple finally retired to the King Suite in the castle. It had been a truly spectacular event and one of which everyone involved could be justly proud. It was the fairytale wedding that Kerry, as a little girl, could hardly have dares to dream about; now, she was not only Mrs McFadden, but a famous celebrity who had just lived her dream.

And she was certainly aware of what a long way she had

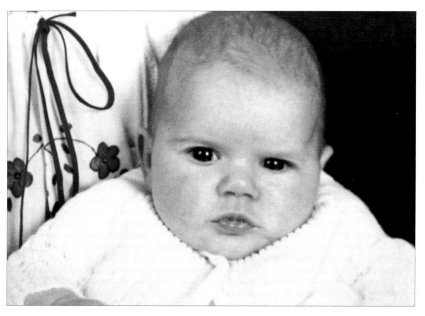

A kitten is born.

Above: Baby Kerry at six months old.

Below left: Even at a young age, she was keen to entertain.

Below right: Kerry and her mother Sue.

A young Kerry with her doting great-grandmother, Blanche.

Even as a young star, she never stopped smiling.

Above left: Strike a pose! Kerry enjoys the limelight of being in front of the camera.

Above right: At school before she set out on the road to fame.

Below: Kerry playing pool with her stepfather, Arnold Ferrier.

Above: On tour with fellow Atomic Kitten bandmates, Liz Mclarnon, *left*, and Natasha Hamilton, *right*.

Below left: A happy Kerry performing on stage.

Below right: Kerry and the band play in a charity football tournament at Wembley.

Kerry at the People's Awards at the Royal Albert Hall in 2000.

Kerry started dating Brian McFadden from Irish band Westlife in 2000. The pair are pictured with the Met Bar's dog, Oscar as they were leaving a nightclub.

Kerry and Brian at the Brit Music Awards 2004.

come. Angela Taylor, her aunt, felt what many did, that it was actually Kerry's tough background that had given her the determination to get from there to here, the centre of attention at the showbiz wedding of the year. 'It made her more determined to succeed – she's done so much in such a short time she almost can't believe it,' she said. 'She's built a nice life for herself with a great career ahead and her own little family – the wedding was the final piece falling into place.'

Kerry herself was bemused. 'I said to my mum, "Can you believe where we are,"' she confessed afterwards. 'We used to live in dingy council flats and I used to be on the dole. I'd thought that I was going to be famous and I've worked and slogged so hard to get what I want – and it's paid off. Now my wedding pictures will be seen by people all over the world. It's mad but it's wonderful.'

And so, finally, the couple were able to embark on their honeymoon. Molly was to stay with Bryan's parents while Kerry and her new husband were away, first travelling to Africa and then on to an island in the Indian Ocean, with their marital status something both were only just getting used to. Spotted at Dublin airport, Kerry quipped, 'It feels really strange. I don't look old enough to buy a packet of cigarettes, let alone be a married woman.' But she was. At just twenty-one, she had a husband, a baby and a blossoming career and was loving every minute of her new life.

The honeymoon itself started in Sun City in South

Africa, where the couple stayed at the sumptuous Lost Palace Hotel, one of the most luxurious hotels in the world. They were soon spotted – not least because Bryan jumped on stage in the hotel's Trader Bar, and staged an impromptu sing-a-long with the band, singing 'Mustang Sally', and also because Westlife were massively famous on the continent. Both were utterly happy, at ease and willing to mingle with the crowds; married life clearly suited both of them.

From there it was on to Mauritius, where the same sunny and informal atmosphere was maintained. Even here, Kerry and Bryan didn't mind being recognised. 'They have been getting on with everyone in the hotel really well,' said a fellow guest. 'They haven't been harassed by fans, but they've been very talkative to everyone they met. Each day they come out of their room around 11.00am and have breakfast by the pool. Then they usually just sunbathe for a couple of hours before going for lunch. They've visited a few of the bars in the evening but they haven't exactly been going party mad. They mingle with all the locals and don't act like big stars at all. Most nights they are in bed by 11.00pm and they usually order a bottle of wine to the bedroom.'

The two continued to behave like besotted teenagers, something highlighted when the couple were seen out on a mini-cruise with a group of other people. 'They were having a very romantic time of it and didn't seem to have a care in the world,' said an onlooker. 'They decided to hire a boat and go out for a day on the ocean and they had a ball. They were hugging and kissing all day and then they went out for a romantic meal. A couple of their mates are also in Mauritius on holiday, so they all decided to meet up for a day out.' It was an idyll that suited them perfectly, to say nothing of allowing the duo the opportunity for some well earned rest.

But it was all over quickly. Given that both Bryan and Kerry had very busy schedules, they were forced to return to Ireland after just over a week away. Both had work to go back to – Bryan to Westlife and Kerry to the television career that was already taking off. Not that it was too onerous a sacrifice to go back, for both had been missing Molly badly. She was still only five months old and, at that age, of course, babies change so quickly, as her proud parents discovered when they were reunited with her. 'We both missed her so much and we'll never go away without her again,' said Kerry on their return.

'Bryan and I had a really romantic time but we missed Molly terribly – we rang at all hours to see how she was. It was so hard to be away from her and, when we got back, she had changed so much I was in tears. Bryan and I went to the hotel to pick her up from our parents and we both ran as fast as we could down the hallway so we could see her. It was such a relief to see her again and Bryan and I made a vow to take her everywhere.'

And now that they were back to what was, for Kerry and Bryan, their normal life, both were beginning to take stock of the wedding. It had been a magnificent affair, as far removed from Kerry's background as it could possibly have been, and it had the effect of bringing her childhood to mind. 'All I kept thinking during the wedding was, "Wow – this is a dream and I'm going to wake up from it soon,"' she said. 'I had quite a hard upbringing in a poor part of Liverpool and it wasn't easy at the best of times. I never thought I'd be the girl at the centre of attention in the biggest wedding of the year.

'I couldn't have been happier on the day because I was marrying the man of my dreams and having the perfect wedding. The wedding was all over the newspapers and TV and I think Bryan and I were both shocked by the size of it all. Everywhere we looked, there were pictures of the church, stories about the wedding dress and everything else to do with it. By the time the big day arrived, we were both very nervous.' But everyone conceded that the day had gone fantastically well.

Indeed, Kerry revealed that she had initially been thinking of quite a different kind of ceremony. 'I originally wanted a small wedding, because I've only got a small family,' she said. 'But Bryan's family is huge so we thought if we were going to have a big wedding, then we'd do it properly – the whole fairytale thing. But I have to say, it was really bizarre when we were in the car coming to the church with my foster-dad and my auntie… I just thought, "This is so weird I can't believe it."'

Much the same could have been said about Kerry's life

to date. Anyone who manages the journey from obscurity to fame knows that the transition can be difficult but, in Kerry's case, that was particularly so. Against all the odds, she had fought against every difficulty life placed before her to succeed in possibly the most difficult field there is – showbusiness.

And she had not just succeeded, she was becoming an object of genuine national affection. Once, in the early days of Atomic Kitten, Kerry had giggled that she had many skeletons hiding in her closet. By this time, they were all out and the public only loved her more for them. Kerry combined vulnerability with inner steel; she refused to apologise for past mistakes and was determined to make the most that life had to offer. And for now, that was settling down as a celebrity, mother... and wife.

7

MUM'S THE WORD

At just twenty-one, Kerry seemed to have it all. She was adapting to the roles of wife and mother fast, on top of which she had a burgeoning career as a television presenter, making programmes from locations all over the world. And although she was still so young, she already had a lifetime of experience behind her, and was ready to expand the family as soon as she could. Her husband felt the same. 'Bryan and I definitely want to have more kids,' she confided about a month after the wedding. 'Being a mum to Molly came so naturally to me and really all I've ever wanted is to be married and have a family.'

Indeed, Kerry finally seemed to have the security that had eluded her for so long. Bryan appeared to be the model husband and father, so what could be more natural than to plan for a larger family? 'Now I've got that – a husband and a daughter – and I couldn't be happier,' Kerry continued. 'And there's no doubt about it – maybe it will be later on in the year or maybe it will be later than that, but we definitely want to have more children. As soon as Bryan and I knew we were having a baby, we were both so overwhelmed. It was a shock to the system, but the first thing Bryan said to me was, "You know, we're going to be great parents." And since then we've been so happy – Molly is the most beautiful girl in the world.' Kerry clearly was really content; she could hardly speak at that point in her life without talking about her adored husband and baby.

But there were very big pressures building within the apparently perfect life the couple were now leading. Apart from constantly being on the go and living to a very tight schedule, every move the duo made was scrutinised and Bryan and Kerry frequently found themselves the subject of as much criticism as they did compliments. This applied to the wedding as much as anything else. The couple admitted that they had had a slightly hard time in the papers because of the sponsorship deal, with some papers carping about the fact that the bride and groom had not allowed their fans to see everything that was going on.

Kerry was not unduly concerned. 'We got slated in the papers but that's only because they didn't get a picture, so the only story they could come up with was one slagging us off,' she said. 'I wasn't too bothered to be honest – it was quite easy to keep away from the press. And as for the reports giving off about the Gardai being on the scene and how it was a waste of taxpayers' money, well, when there are members of the public involved in large numbers, the Gardai are always there to make sure no one gets hurt. We didn't say, "We're celebrities, we need this and we need that" – it was because there were so many fans involved and they were worried about their safety.'

But there were signs of stress emerging. One day, as she was staying in London, Kerry started suffering from severe stomach pains. She was rushed to Chelsea and Westminster Hospital, where she was found to have a cyst the size of a football. It was hastily removed, although it was discovered to be non-malignant and the alarm passed. It was a nasty shock, however, and a clear physical sign that Kerry's non-stop lifestyle was taking its toll.

'Kerry was in a lot of pain… I'm very relieved it's all over,' said Bryan afterwards. 'The operation has been a complete success and she's slowly starting to get back on her feet. But she is going to need to take at least a month off work to recover.' Indeed, it was fortunate that the cyst was discovered when it was. 'It was very worrying for us,' said Bryan. 'The worst thing they told us was that, if they had not discovered it for another week, it might have been fatal.

'So, she spent three days in the hospital and thankfully they let her out just before the weekend. This week she has been resting in a London hotel as I've been away in Poland with the band. But she was able to make it on Wednesday night for the Brits, which was great as we won the Best Pop Act and it was great to have her there for it.' Despite there being some discord between Bryan and the band So Solid Crew, this did not spoil the evening and the incident was quickly forgotten.

Other niggles also refused to go away. Bryan continued to speak about the coverage the wedding had received; unlike Kerry, he seemed more defensive about the churlishness from some quarters, especially about the amount the couple had received in payment from *Hello!* magazine. 'If the truth were known, we actually lost money on our wedding,' he protested.

'The *Hello!* deal paid us £300,000, but the whole wedding and honeymoon cost us £400,000. The tabloids all slated everything we did about the wedding. They even slagged us off for asking the guests to donate money to charity instead of giving us presents. Don't get me wrong – it was wonderful and the magazine was great to us.'

The tone was a bit unfortunate, given that the two had just returned from honeymoon. But clearly the griping rankled and Bryan later complained that the cost had been higher still than he had at first realised. 'When we returned to Ireland [from the honeymoon], we were told that the bill for our wedding was over budget by £200,000 – can you believe it?' he said a couple of months on. 'There was a free bar and most of our family and friends are alcoholics so you can imagine 350 people drinking away.' He was joking, but the message was clear – he was getting tired of the brickbats that seem to go along with modern-day celebrity.

Even Kerry felt a little dissatisfied on their return from the honeymoon. It's common for a newly married couple to feel a sense of anti-climax in the wake of the celebrations, and how much more must that feeling be if the entire country had been watching your nuptials with interest? 'The actual day was fantastic, but the build-up was better,' she confessed. 'I didn't feel that emotional during the ceremony – just giddy.' Again, the stress seemed to be taking its toll.

The come-down from the wedding wasn't that easy, either. 'It was so depressing,' Kerry admitted. 'I remember sitting in the car on the way back to Dublin waiting for Bryan to get fish and chips and I had a face like thunder. I remember thinking, "It's all over." We went back to our apartment and the heating wasn't working. Then we flew to South Africa, but didn't realise how famous Bryan was there, so we couldn't move out of our hotel. We later flew to Mauritius where no one knew us – but everyone was over 50.' Of course, the couple had actually appeared blissfully happy on honeymoon – it was just the aftermath of all the excitement that was plunging the duo into a slightly tetchy mood.

And quite apart from all the comment about the wedding ceremony, Bryan was fretting about money in other ways, too. The couple had put their country home in Co Wicklow on the market just over six months after buying it for £1.2 million; they now learned that it might fetch no more than £800,000. 'We could lose about

£400,000, which is a lot of money, no matter how much you've got,' he fretted.

'It is a lovely house and we loved it when we found it, but Kerry hated living there. She got lonely and found it a bit creepy and large. There was just an old woman in a house over the road and her and that was it for miles.' Indeed, the couple had now decided definitively to make Dublin their home; they were currently knocking two penthouses into one in Donaghmede. But money can't have been too much of a worry for the McFaddens – Bryan had already announced that when his next royalty cheque came in, he was going to purchase a Ferrari.

Kerry was also relieved to be in Dublin. She had grown up in a city and found the countryside not quite right for her. 'We like to be near the city where everything is happening,' she said. 'We tried living out in a big house in the countryside, but it wasn't for us. In the end, we wanted to get back to what we knew and we bought a nice place in the city. We are a really normal family, and just do normal things when we are at home. We spend most of our time playing with Molly and going out on family trips.

'I didn't have an easy childhood but I knew the value of love and how important that is. That's the most important thing to me – giving love to Molly, and it doesn't matter how much money you have, love is what really counts. I don't know what I want her to be when she grows up but I would be happy for her no matter what path she chooses, as long as she's happy.' It was a touching remark: Kerry might now be enjoying material success in life, but she had never let it become a way of spoiling her daughter.

Their home life was actually similar to many newly married couples. Asked if Bryan was any good at housework, Kerry replied, 'Are you having a laugh? As far as housework is concerned, Bryan takes his plate out when he's finished his dinner. And that's after much convincing to get him off the Playstation so that I can watch *Corrie* and *EastEnders* – so often I miss the soaps because he's playing whatever his favourite game is. And when you ask Bryan to make the bed – well, he tries. But I have to say, he's brilliant with Molly – housework, no, but with Molly, it's a different story.'

And Kerry was certainly happy. Bryan, too, was also clearly as enamoured of Kerry as ever. Back from the honeymoon, he was keen to make it clear that their life together was as full as ever, while drooling over his new wife's natural assets. 'After the baby's born, it takes a while to get back into your old routine, but we're there now!' he said. 'Everyone says I must have been first attracted to Kerry's boobs, but I didn't even know she had a great body until about a week after I met her.

'It was her face and eyes and the fact that she was so cute and bubbly. Kerry does have quite a large chest – if she wears low-cut tops, she doesn't always look her best, so I have said things like, "I don't think that top suits you." That look doesn't turn me on. It's much sexier to see just the shape of a woman's breasts through a top – it leaves more to the imagination. She was radiant when she was pregnant. The sexiest part of her was her bump, which was so sexy.'

And so, for the time being, all was well. The nation was as supportive of Kerry as ever; indeed, in March 2003, she beat off stiff competition from Victoria Beckham, Cherie Blair and Kate Winslet to be named British celebrity mother of the year. Kerry was both shocked and thrilled. 'I am overwhelmed people voted for me, absolutely delighted,' she said when she went to pick up her award, having taken her own mother along with her for the day. 'All I wanted was to have my own family. I didn't know about this until a couple of days ago and everyone thought Victoria would win, but I did, instead. Sorry. I want another baby. I love kids.' Molly had clearly brought her a whole new layer of fulfilment that had become more important to her than anything else.

Asked for her advice on the subject of good motherhood, Kerry was quite clear about her secret; she and Molly were practically inseparable. Indeed, they went everywhere together. 'Don't read any of the books,' she said, 'it's a load of nonsense. I thought, "I'm not going to be able to look after this little human being," but it's the best thing I've ever done, better than being at Number One. Molly is a daddy's girl. Bryan is brilliant with her. He was bad at getting up in the night at first, but he dotes on her.'

Her win as Mother of the Year was a sign of quite how popular Kerry now was. Up to 10,000 people had voted in the poll, carried out by bluefootbear.com, and a number of the people involved were in no doubt as to why she had won. 'Kerry had a bit of a hard childhood after foster care and I believe she has struck a chord with people by the way she has bounced back,' said Alicia Tindall, spokeswoman for the company.

Rajesh Shah, the teddy firm's boss, had a different theory. 'People respect the fact that she gave up her pop career to have a family, even though the group had just had a Number One,' he said. In truth, it was a combination of all these factors – deprived childhood, besotted parent and strong personality – that put Kerry at the top of the list.

Kerry was, however, also beginning to get her career back on track. Shortly after returning from honeymoon, Kerry was signed up to co-host a Childline concert with Nicky Byrne, as well as acting as a roving reporter for Channel Five's *Exclusive*. 'I've performed on Childline before but I have never hosted anything like this – it will be my first big live presenting role,' she said.

'Presenting is definitely what I want to do and maybe a bit of acting. At the moment, Molly's too young and I don't want to leave her, but with presenting I can pick and choose what jobs I do which gives me time to spend with her.' She also said that she enjoyed the role of interviewer. 'I have to say, though, I've just interviewed Westlife for *Exclusive* and that was bizarre,' she added. 'Interviewing your own husband is really weird.'

By April, she had already been signed up to present the

Channel 5 show *Exclusive*, and was in talks to front a dating show, *Elimidate*, on ITV1. But that meant that she and Bryan again had schedules that were as frantic as ever, as both spent an increasingly longer time away from home to do their work. There was, however, no alternative; this is what a successful career in showbiz entailed. 'There's so much of the time that Bryan and I have to spend apart and that's the hardest thing,' said Kerry.

'He will be away working with Westlife and I'll be in London doing my TV work and it becomes heartbreaking. I take Molly everywhere with me because I want to be there for every second of her growing up. But the time it really hits home is when you're sitting on your own in the evening and the baby is sleeping. That's when I miss Bryan most. I love him as much as the day we got married and it's hard for us. It's tough for Bryan, too, because he has to go all over the world with Westlife and misses some of the little things with Molly. He'll be on the phone to us for hours when he is away, just talking about things.

'Some times we go for weeks spending every minute together, but with my TV work it's become more difficult to coordinate our schedules. But the bottom line for Bryan and me is that we put our family first. He is a family man and that comes before everything. Whenever we get to even spend an hour together, one of us will jump on the plane and make that journey. We don't want to be one of those couples that makes a bit of money, then just sits doing nothing for the rest of our lives. We are prepared to work.'

That was an understatement; given that both were new parents as well as very hard-working celebrities, their dedication at that time would have put anyone to shame. And Bryan was not averse to turning up whenever he could to surprise Kerry, as he had done before they were married. On one occasion, when Kerry appeared on the karaoke show *Night Fever*, hosted by Suggs from Madness, Bryan smuggled himself into the audience wearing a fake beard and straw hat. He remained undetected throughout.

One thing Kerry was not yet ready to do, however, was to go out on stage on her own. Television presenting was one thing, but singing was quite another, and she made it clear she was simply not ready to take that step. 'I just can't handle having to go out on that stage all on my own,' she said. 'It was different when I was in Atomic Kitten and the other girls were with me. Plenty of people have offered to give me a record deal and invited me to perform at concerts, but I really don't think I could do it.'

There was also, of course, Molly to consider. It is easier to combine parenting with television presenting than with a life as a pop star, something Kerry was very aware of. 'I'd never say never, but I'm really happy presenting, so I can't see myself joining a band,' she said. 'Also, I don't want to leave Molly at home and touring is very tough. It's hard enough with Bryan being away without me doing the same. And when she starts school, my work will have to fit in with her. I always want to be there for her.'

The bond between mother and daughter was growing

stronger by the day and Kerry was also able to do at least some travelling with her. 'I took Molly with me as often as I could on *Elimidate*,' she recounted. 'She came to the Bahamas, Iceland and Sun City and she loved it. I took her swimming and she got loads of fuss from everyone.' Molly, like her parents, was growing up to be a very well travelled little girl.

As for the show itself, Kerry was proud of what the team had produced. 'I'm really excited about this show,' she had said, shortly after signing up for the series. 'It's going to be full of outrageous fun.' Now that filming was completed, she and the producers were happy with the finished product. 'The show will be on late at night as it's a bit risqué,' she revealed. 'It was hard work and we had very long days filming.' But it was worthwhile, not least because it was giving Kerry her first proper experience at fronting a show. As for the show itself – well, it wasn't actually a great success, being pulled from the schedule after six outings. But it was a start.

Another concern was regaining her figure after the birth of Molly. Kerry has always had an envious figure, going at different times from curvy to, in more recent years, super-slim, but even she worried about getting back in shape. 'There are times when I thought I'd never get back to the way I was,' she admitted. 'I think everyone who has a baby worries about their weight after it's all over, because there is a fear that you'll never be your old self again. But I'm happy with the way I look and so is Bryan, which is the most important thing. He always tells me that he prefers the way I am now and also that he likes a bit of meat on a girl. I think people can get too hung up on weight and in showbiz there's always focus on how people look and that can be hard.'

It was something that Kerry dwelt on, however. She had been famous for some years now, and realised that, as a public figure, she was almost bound to be photographed wherever she went. This had its own stresses and strains that she, like every woman in the business, was only too aware of. 'I was only six-and-a-half stone when I was first in the band, but I had such a large bust that I don't think I ever looked really skinny,' she said.

'I put on four stone when I was pregnant and I'm only 5 foot 3 inches. I got stretch marks on my hips and lots of my hair fell out. And, worst of all, I had terrible bleeding gums every time I brushed my teeth, but apparently that's very common when you're pregnant. After leaving Atomic Kitten and having Molly, my body has changed shape and Bryan says he prefers it. He says men don't like stick-thin women and that we're supposed to have curves.'

And curves she certainly had. Kerry had hired a personal trainer to help her get back in shape, but had discovered, to her bemusement, that her bust size had grown and refused to go down. 'I was a DD cup before I got pregnant, but the people at *Elimidate* said I looked like I was wearing the wrong size,' she said slightly bashfully. 'I couldn't believe it when I found out I'm now an FF.'

Actually, Kerry was not the only one worrying about her figure. Bryan later revealed that he had received a phone call when they were still on honeymoon from a notoriously waspish member of the showbiz community... Simon Cowell. 'I told him that's the way I am,' he related on television afterwards. 'I'm not going to have any liposuction. He couldn't ruin my honeymoon. He did phone me but it didn't spoil my holiday. Nothing Simon Cowell says could spoil my honeymoon. This is how I am and I'm happy with it. I don't want to change for anybody. I don't disrespect him for the way he does it. He's just being honest.'

Of course, Westlife were still as active as ever and, banter aside, there was a real chance that all of them would be put on strict diet and exercise programmes. They had not yet cracked the United States, but neither had they given up hopes of doing so and were aware that their image had to be just right. Bryan didn't just have a healthy appetite, though – he was also a great one for a drink and, when the boys were on tour on Oslo, was tracked down to a nightclub enjoying his eleventh beer of the evening. He was in a mellow mood.

'I've always loved a drink and have spent quite a bit on nights out, but hey, you work hard and you play hard,' he said. 'I've also bought three houses in the last year, but sold one of them recently. Obviously, my daughter Molly is taken care of for the future, but I still like to spend money on things for my wife, Kerry, my parents and my friends.

It's nice to do things like that once in a while.' He could afford to – the boys were said to be earning £2 million each from the tour.

And so, Kerry and Bryan settled into their new life, getting used to their marital status and forging ahead with their careers. Everything seemed to be going well for both of them; after Kerry's health scare, both were now on top form and eager to tackle many more projects in the future. But the honeymoon was about to come to an abrupt end, in the most brutal way possible, with a shock that no one could have expected. An event that had taken place months previously suddenly resurfaced, with the most devastating consequences. Kerry and Bryan had barely been married five months before a crisis occurred that threatened the very foundations of their marriage.

8

A KITTEN SHOWS
HER CLAWS

The news, when it came, was totally unexpected. Kerry and Bryan, widely considered to be one of showbusiness's strongest couples, had been married for less than five months when the bombshell erupted. Bryan – besotted, loving, and a perfect husband – found himself at the centre of some very sordid revelations. Amy Barker, a lap-dancer who had been present at Bryan's stag night three months before the wedding took place, had a decidedly unsavoury story to tell.

It seemed that what had happened was that Amy, a mother-of-two from Wakefield, West Yorkshire, and another lap-dancer, had been hired to entertain Westlife on a coach trip from Dublin to Limerick on 28 October 2001. Another forty guests were there, including Dane Bowers, the drink flowed, everyone ended up at Lapello's club in

Limerick, and what the papers used to coyly term a 'sex act' took place. Actually, that is what it eventually turned out to be – the original reports made it sound much worse. Initially, she had gone along with Bryan's desperate attempt to keep the whole episode quiet, but finally, she told all.

Kerry was filming in the Bahamas when the story broke. She was working on the television show *Elimidate* and was turning out to be a TV natural; her new career was already blossoming. This, however, was a crisis of the first order and, very unusually, the producers gave her a few days off to have heart-to-heart with Bryan, a 48-hour pass on 'compassionate grounds'. Bryan himself was alternating between fury and bluster. 'People are blowing it all out of proportion,' he snapped. 'Everything is going to be OK… it's all been taken out of context. I have spoken to Kerry.'

But actions speak louder than words. Kerry had not, yet, said anything openly about what had happened, but she certainly didn't appear to be as calm as Bryan's words suggested. Rather than going to Las Vegas, as her filming schedule dictated, she got on the first plane to London, transferring from there to Newcastle-upon-Tyne, to confront her erring spouse. Neither were her friends making light of the situation, describing her as 'shocked and devastated'.

A source on the show saw what had happened. 'She got on the first flight out of the Bahamas to England so she could get the truth from Bryan,' he said. 'The show producer gave her a couple of days to try to get things sorted. They didn't have a lot of time because the film crew were waiting for Kerry in Vegas. Her contract doesn't allow her to interrupt the filming schedule, which has taken her to loads of different countries.

'It's an unusual move to let Kerry leave because of the possible loss of money and time, but the producer obviously realised Kerry needed to get this sorted before she could concentrate fully on her filming. He's from the North and knows the importance placed on family. He immediately gave Kerry a couple of days and continued filming what he could without her. He says she's an absolutely brilliant TV host and really gets the best out of the contestants. He says she is the best he has worked with and he obviously wanted to do everything in his power to help her at this time.'

For Kerry, it must have been absolutely shattering. Not only had she had no idea at all that anything like this might have happened, but she had also believed that, with Bryan, she had finally found the security that had eluded her for so long. And, after all, there was no reason she shouldn't have believed that; Bryan himself had lost no opportunity publicly to avow his love for her, not only in telling the rest of the world how he felt about her, but also in writing songs for her, talking about their future together and telling everyone she was the perfect women. It must have seemed utterly cruel to Kerry that, so soon after her marriage, a crisis such as this one arose.

It did not take Bryan long to realise the gravity of the

situation. Out went the bluster and in came abject apologies to his extremely upset wife. Westlife still had their performances to do and so Bryan had to go along with them, but he was visibly moved when he sang 'Bop Bop Baby', a song he had written for Kerry, at the Sheffield Arena. 'That was the hardest performance I've ever done,' he said afterwards. 'When I was singing it, all I could think about was Kerry. I love her so much.'

Indeed, he was clearly full of remorse, calling it, in the well-worn phrase, a 'moment of madness'. 'I'm really sorry for what happened,' he said. 'I was such an idiot. Kerry and I sat down together and talked about everything. She went mad and I don't blame her but we've promised to put it behind us and get on with our lives. I'm so lucky having Kerry and our daughter Molly. Kerry has been very understanding and I'm so lucky to have a wife like that. I'll never put anyone through this hurt ever again. We will get through this and carry on being a happy family.' But he was clearly very shocked at the full extent of the upset he had caused.

At first, Kerry was also clear that this would not break them apart. Her first public statement came when she was spotted going through Heathrow: 'Look, it's still there,' she said, pointing to her wedding ring. 'There are no problems. I am madly in love with Bryan and Bryan is madly in love with me. Everything is behind us.' And off she went, putting a brave face on it. She had a career to attend to, after all.

Bryan himself continued to try to make amends. He

continued to proclaim his love for Kerry in public, as well as dong everything he could behind the scenes to make up for it. 'Myself and Kerry are more in love than ever,' he proclaimed, as matters finally began to subside. 'She did fly to the UK to see me. But Kerry is always backward and forward to me and our daughter Molly when she is filming. We are not splitting up or anything of the sort. She has flown back now to finish her TV show in the Bahamas. After that she is going to film in Las Vegas. Then she will fly to Mauritius to finish filming. Then she is flying back to Molly and me. She will join me on tour with Westlife until we travel back to Dublin on June 6th in the Point.' Both parties seemed determined to carry on just as they had done before.

But the ring issue, rather unfortunately, reared its head again almost immediately, this time when Bryan appeared on GMTV without wearing his. There was an immediate furore, with intensive speculation as to whether they had, indeed, split up after all. Bryan's management assured everyone that all was well and that a diamond had fallen out, so that he had sent it away for repair. They had been spotted earlier in the week all over one another at an Enrique Iglesias concert, so there seemed a chance, at least, that everything was calming down.

Kerry, incidentally, was none too impressed by the Spanish star. Her life might have been turned upside-down, but she was still capable of making her own assessment of her colleagues in her own inimitable way. 'I met Enrique Iglesias the other night after his concert,' she recalled afterwards. 'Me and Bryan went for a drink with him and he's really boring. I asked him how old he was and he looked at me oddly as if I should already have known.'

He wasn't the only one Kerry felt rather dubious about; at around the same time, she recalled being on *SM:tv* with Atomic Kitten and Geri Halliwell just after reading Geri's autobiography. 'I had read her book and thought she sounded down-to-earth, so I said, "I'm going to knock at her door." A bloke opened it and I asked, "Is Geri there?" No one had a clue who I was. I said, "I'm in a new girl band. Can I say hello?" I heard Geri say, "Tell her to go away, I'm getting my make-up done." That was it, then, I washed my hands of her. What harm would it have done to pop her head round and say, "Hiya?" Who cares if she's got no make-up on? In half the shows I've done, I'm not wearing make-up and I've never brushed my hair.'

Back with the crew of *Elimidate*, Kerry was determined to put on a professional appearance. She was accompanied by her good friend Michelle Hunter, who was clearly an invaluable source of support. Kerry was, however, desperately upset. 'These last few days haven't been the best of times,' she said in an interview at the time, during which she wore sunglasses to hide her swollen eyes. 'But at the end of the day, me and Bryan, we are a family. And the situation is about more than just us. There's a baby involved who we both love very much.'

There was a massive feeling of sympathy building for

Kerry. Despite being in circumstances that would be devastating for anyone, particularly if it all took place in the glare of the public eye, Kerry remained the natural, unaffected woman she had always been, right down to apologising for those dark glasses. 'I'm sorry I'm sitting here with my sunglasses on,' she said. 'I hope you don't think I'm being a stuck-up showbiz star or anything like that. It's just that I'm really jet-lagged and this whole horrible situation with Bryan is really getting to me. My head isn't here at the moment. I'm all over the place. I hope you understand. I'm a professional. At the end of the day, I'm doing my job. I'm just trying to get on with it. But you'll appreciate it's not easy. I'd rather be concentrating on my home life, but I've made a commitment.'

But behind the scenes, Kerry was very far from forgiving Bryan – in actual fact, she was so furious that there were rumours the two were indeed going to split up. Kerry had had no idea a story like this was about to break; as far as she had known, she and Bryan had been a happy and loving couple. And now this story had surfaced, so soon after the wedding, too. But she was also aware that it was not just between her and Bryan any more; Molly was also an issue. She was not yet a year old; it was an appalling dilemma in which to find herself. But what should she do?

'She is not sure that she can trust Bryan any more,' said a source who was close to her at the time. 'To be unfaithful on his stag do, when she had only just had their baby Molly, does not bode well for the future of their marriage.

Kerry has always been determined to have a real family because she had a difficult upbringing but this has shattered all her illusions. Bryan spouted to all and sundry about how Kerry is the love of his life and Molly has made him grow up. But Kerry is now beginning to wonder whether that was all empty rubbish.

'She is seething and there have been some extremely angry telephone calls between Vegas and Newcastle. He claims it was a one-off and that he was extremely drunk. She is saying if he can do it once, then he can easily do it again. They are apart a lot of the time and Kerry knows if she can't trust him completely, her mind will never be at rest.'

Bryan was clearly distraught at what he had done but, even so, he ended up doing what so many celebrities who have been caught out have resorted to – he blamed it all on the press. 'The press build you up and they love making you a success, but as soon as you're there and there's no more they can do for you, they just want to take you down,' he said. 'It's the same with everybody. They're going to do it to me and do it to everybody. You've just got to learn to live with it. You've got to learn to be yourself and keep your private life and work life separate and ignore anyone else. It is tough but that's life. It's all part of the job. It's what we ask for.'

This line of complaint continued, that while it was a personal problem between the couple, media attention made it very much worse to deal with. Undoubtedly, this was the case, but then Bryan, like any celebrity, knew that there were two sides to this coin – he needed media attention to stay in the public eye, and yet he didn't enjoy it when it became negative. It is a balance every modern celebrity has to fight to get right and, just at this point, Bryan was not enjoying the massive exposure his actions had prompted. But he knew it was the downside of a relationship with the press that could also be very positive for him when life was going according to plan.

But that knowledge didn't help either of them. Over six weeks after the revelations first broke, Bryan gave an interview in which he admitted that the two had had huge rows about what had happened. 'There was fighting and stuff as the two of us got together and tried to deal with it,' he said. 'But it was harder trying to deal with other people. They kept coming up to us to ask if it was true. I told them it was exaggerated. Everyone has tiffs and arguments at home, but it makes me feel sore towards the media because, before that story broke, we didn't have this sort of friction to deal with.

'Kerry and I were always together through the whole thing and the support we had from the boys and our families helped us get through it. Kerry and I have strong relationships with our families. The revelation about that lap-dancer couldn't have come at a worse time for me, because I was in the middle of a Westlife tour. It snowballed into a big, stupid thing.

'The hard part was reading about it every day and getting

over it. It came up so much. I just wanted it to go away. The difficult part wasn't about explaining to Kerry so much as having to face other people, who would come and ask me about it. Kerry is a very strong person. A lot of things happened, but it has brought us closer together. It was the kind of thing our relationship had to go through because I'm in a band.'

But the two were trying to put it behind them, so much so that there were rumours that Kerry was pregnant again. Bryan denied this, although he was clearly hoping that he soon would be a father again. 'She hasn't told me there's another kid on the way,' he said. 'Not that I know of. Trying for a baby is the best part, though. We've been practising for a while and it'll be a while yet before we decide to have another kid. It's great to go home at night and be with Molly. It's brilliant. I love coming home to the family rather than having to stay in a hotel.'

Kerry was increasingly beginning to be able to talk about the revelations publicly, too, lashing out at the woman involved. 'What kind of a woman would do something like that?' she demanded. 'We've only been married for five months, and there's a baby involved, too. You've got to be a bit sick, I'm afraid, to do that and then get paid for it. I'm sorry, but I think she's very disturbed to do that to a marriage.' She was still clearly quite furious at what had occurred, not least because although she had had to endure aspects of her past life being exposed, she had never had to cope with a situation like this before.

And so Kerry and Bryan determined to overcome what had gone wrong. Both were sounding increasingly keen to have another child: 'Yes, I want more kids,' said Bryan, shortly after the furore. 'I haven't discussed numbers with Kerry yet, but we are trying for more at the moment and we would love to give little Molly a brother or sister… sooner, rather than later.'

Kerry, of course, remained as besotted with Molly as ever; the fact that she had taken so easily to motherhood became more plain than ever. 'I love her to bits, but she's completely daddy's girl,' she said. 'Sometimes if Bryan has got to go and I go, "Come on!" and hold out my arms to her, she won't let go of him. But if I've got her, she's like, "Da-Da!"'

Indeed, Kerry was turning out to be a wonderful mother. She took Molly around the world with her as much as possible, but at the same time kept her feet on the ground and resolutely refused to spoil her. Molly's first birthday would probably be celebrated while her parents were on tour with Westlife, said Kerry, while flatly turning down the idea of a lavish birthday party of the type thrown by the Beckhams.

'The tour will be in America and me and Bryan will probably take her out for the day,' said Kerry. When asked about the idea of throwing a Beckham-style party, she responded, 'It's ridiculous. I'm sorry, it is. For a one-year-old child? I think it was more for the parents than anybody. I remember at Christmas, we got all these presents for

Molly – a swinging chair, a walker and stuff like that – but because she was just four months old she was more interested in the wrapping paper. So this year, that's all I'm buying her – wrapping paper.'

But Bryan's transgressions was still playing badly on her mind. Once the initial shock was over, Kerry declared herself ready to forgive him, although she certainly could not be said to be happy about what had happened. 'Bryan knows he's done wrong, but we're going to try and put it all behind us,' she said. 'This is just about the worst experience I've been through. We've got to think of Molly. Westlife won't last for ever and my career won't last for ever. I'm trying to plan ahead. We're not the first couple to have problems and we won't be the last. Bryan and I will survive this [but] I'm not going to lie and say it's been easy.'

There were, at least, plenty of other distractions in Kerry's life to help take her mind off it. Her television career was going really well; apart from the stint on *This Morning* with Bryan – 'It was fun and I enjoyed working with him, but I prefer to do my own thing,' she said – there had been successful appearances on *SM:tv* and *CD:UK* with Cat Deeley and a regular slot on *Liquid News* with the late Christopher Price. And above all, of course, there was *Elimidate*, which at first looked as if it was proving to be a great success. It was about survival of the fittest in the dating game; four girls would battle it out over one boy and vice versa, in some of the world's most spectacular locations. To date, Kerry had travelled to the Bahamas and

Las Vegas, as well as Mauritius and Sun City where, of course, she had also been on honeymoon.

And she was loving it, despite all the problems involved. There had also been a trip to Kenya, which Kerry found enthralling – despite some fears about the local wildlife. 'My room was on the ground floor,' she recounted. 'What's going to stop a lion coming on to my balcony at six in the morning? Nothing! So the first night, I ended up sleeping in Vanessa the assistant producer's room, which was two floors up.'

Kerry also found Africa's insects difficult to cope with – which was ironic, given what was to become one of her greatest successes – but she had already had some practice in overcoming her fears. Giving an interview in mid-2002, Kerry recalled, 'Last year, I did Children in Need in Belfast and I had to raise £55,000 or I'd have to let a tarantula walk up my arm. So I raised the money and thought I'd got away with it. But then someone in the crowd stood up and said, 'I'll give you £1,800 if you get that tarantula to walk up your arm.' It was live TV… I couldn't refuse.' There was no question at all about it – the girl had a lot of guts.

But the filming schedule took its toll, especially at such a stressful time in Kerry's life. It was ironic that one of the reasons she had left Atomic Kitten had been because she was tiring of the incessant travelling, for *Elimidate* had made her schedule busier than ever. 'It's been very hard not being with my family,' she said, when she was six weeks into an eight-week stint. 'Very difficult. It's been non-stop, go, go, go. I don't know what day it is, I don't know what time zone it is. I haven't had a break at all. I didn't know the show would be so long. It's been eight weeks non-stop, but it's good for my career and it's been a good chance to see the world.'

And she wasn't just missing her family, she was also desperate to see her friends, too. Her erstwhile colleague in Atomic Kitten, Natasha Hamilton, had recently announced her pregnancy and Kerry was clearly rather cut up about not being able to see her in person. 'I spoke to her when I was back in Britain,' she said. 'I'm really missing her. I can't believe I haven't even seen her bump, I'm so upset about it. I'll go and see her as soon as I get back.'

But that down-to-earth quality remained. Kerry, because of her brief stint in a chippy, was chosen to launch a Fish and Chip Shop of the Year Competition, and was adamant that her tastes, despite her fame and wealth, hadn't changed: 'I only ate chips the whole time I was away,' she confessed.

Life returned to normal, of a sort, but there was no doubt that the recent problems had taken their toll. More grumblings about Bryan's behaviour began to emerge – this time from none other than sources close to Westlife. Bryan's behaviour – and not just this recent crisis – was seemingly becoming a little too wild for a group marketed at a young audience, and he was even letting his wild-boy antics spill over on stage, at one point trying to drop his trousers in the middle of a concert in Belfast. His fellow band members didn't appreciate this. Shane branded it

'unprofessional', before add
funny to the audience, but i

He was not the only one
the first moment Kerry had
rumours, always denied, that
drink and now these rumou
than ever. 'Things have been
since the incident with the S〔 〕ew at the Brit
Awards,' said a source close to the band. 'We have let a lot
of things pass with Bryan, like his wild nights with Kerry,
because that's their private life. But when he starts acting
up on stage, that is something else. Their image is their
future and if they start losing fans because of Bryan, then
they put that at risk.'

If truth be told, Bryan's childish behaviour was almost
certainly as a result of the strain he was under. The lap-
dancer revelations had come after, quite literally, years of
hard work, and he was exhausted by everything that had
happened, not just in the recent past but in all the years
since Westlife had become famous. And it really did look as
if Kerry had forgiven him now; the two were often seen
together and appeared to be calming down. They also
talked about another baby more than ever. 'I want more
kids now,' Bryan said in June 2002. 'All together, I would
like three or four kids, but that's just me. I haven't discussed
numbers with Kerry yet but we are trying for more kids at
the moment and we would love to give little Molly a
brother or sister sooner rather than later.

ything else, as soon as we finish the tour I'm
ake Kerry and Molly away on an exotic holiday
what has happened over the past few months out of
ur hair. Kerry is still working on her TV career so we will
have to make time for the break, which we will as soon as
the tour ends. To be honest, I can't wait because I'm
knackered at this stage.'

He wasn't the only one. As spring wore on, Kerry was
again rushed to hospital, this time to Mount Carmel in
Dublin, with problems relating to the cyst she had had
removed earlier in the year. This time it was not so serious,
she had to stay in for only one night, but it was an
indication of the stress she, too, was under.

But that stress was soon to be alleviated for, after a truly
awful six months, a period Kerry and Bryan were desperate
to put behind them, they received some great news.
Indeed, the rumours were true and the two were about to
be granted something both were desperate for – Kerry was
expecting another baby.

9

SISTER ACT

Kerry and Bryan were thrilled. It had been a rotten few months for the couple, casting a black shadow over what should have been a wonderfully happy time together at the start of their marriage. But all that was about to change. Both had spoken frequently about their desire for a second baby for some time and now, although it hadn't been planned, that baby was on her way. It marked a new beginning. All recent troubles could be put behind them; Kerry and Bryan were now able to concentrate on what lay ahead.

Recent medical troubles had taken their toll, however and, when the news broke, Kerry was still not quite at her best. She had put off making the announcement until she was sure everything was all right, which meant that not only had she been feeling dreadful, but that she had had to make up excuses for it. Of course, many expectant mothers don't like to talk about their pregnancies too early, but Kerry didn't have to conceal it simply from family and friends – she had the whole world of showbiz to contend with.

'The past few weeks have been really hard for me, as I have been feeling really ill and having to tell everyone I've got a stomach bug,' she admitted shortly after news of the pregnancy was announced. 'The main reason I didn't want to tell anyone until after I made it to the three-month stage was that I had an operation to remove a cyst from my stomach when I was pregnant. At one stage, I was in so much pain they thought it might be an ectopic pregnancy, but luckily it wasn't and the baby's fine.'

Coincidentally, the baby had been conceived at the Conrad Hotel in London, just as Molly had been. 'It's amazing but it's true,' said Bryan. 'Let that be a warning to any couple staying in room 308 at London's Chelsea Conrad Hotel. Westlife were in London on tour and Kerry had come to see me for the night before flying back to Dublin. A month ago, she started feeling sick.

'We got a home pregnancy test and when Kerry came out of the bathroom smiling, we screamed and hugged each other. It was the best feeling – just like when we knew we were going to have Molly. We can't wait for our new addition.' In actual fact, of course, the Conrad was becoming a home from home away for the McFaddens whenever they were in London, given that they no longer had a flat in the capital. Perhaps the Conrad was not such a surprising location for the addition to the McFadden dynasty, after all.

And, like Molly, this baby, due to be born in February 2003, was a surprise. Both parents, however, saw great advantages in having two young children so close together. 'We wanted another one, but we didn't actually plan it this soon,' Kerry said. 'It's great, though, as they will be so close in age that hopefully they will get along and do everything together. My auntie has two children and there are 18 months between them and they're thick as thieves, so it's nice to get them done and dusted and out of the way.'

With the advent of a second baby, Kerry and Bryan were also on the move again. They had decided that their penthouse apartment was not really suitable for children, so they bought a six-bedroom house nearby in order to bring up their growing brood with the intention of making this one, finally, their family home. Molly had just been christened, and Kerry's television career continued to do well. She had just been signed up for a programme called *Britain's Sexiest*, which aimed to find the man and woman who were exactly that.

Kerry was excited about her new role. 'My agent rang me about it and I thought it sounded fantastic,' she said. 'I had also heard who I was co-presenting it with. I've met [ex–*EastEnders* star] Michael Greco a few times before and he's so lovely. I am really looking forward to it – I get a chance to meet some hunky men, including lots of men in fireman's uniforms, so I couldn't pass that up!'

Her appearance on the show was also a sign of her continuing work ethic. Even though she was pregnant and Bryan was earning more than enough for both of them, Kerry was in no doubt that she wished to continue in her new career. 'Being pregnant is not a disability – look at Davina McCall,' she said. 'She was running around on *Big Brother*. This career will not last for ever and neither will Bryan's. I've got to milk it while I can so I can send my kids to a good school, buy them nice clothes, take them on good holidays and let them live in a nice house.'

Home life also seemed to be happy. The two were getting on very well again and Kerry related how, when she wasn't well, Bryan tended to her, just as he had done in the past. 'We just have such a laugh – he is always looking after me,' she said. 'Today, I was lying on the couch feeling unwell and he just played me a song on the guitar. And then I was too poorly to go into town to get myself a christening outfit so he went and bought some gorgeous clothes.' He was certainly an attentive husband, determined that Kerry's pregnancy should go as well as it could.

Indeed, Kerry was talking again about how loving he could be. 'He's caring, romantic, funny,' she said. 'We'll be watching TV at home and he'll just get up, put one of our favourite Dr Hook songs on and pull me up to dance. One night, he took me out as a surprise and we stayed in a hotel afterwards. The next morning, he had to leave for work but later there was a knock on the door. It was a dozen red roses with a card saying, "Morning, Sweetheart." The following morning, the same thing happened.

'We speak all the time on the phone when we're apart and if I forget to say I love him, he'll phone me straight back and say, "Did you forget to say something?" He makes me feel so, so special. He is a diamond. I love him so much – he is my knight in shining armour. He took me away from the life I led and said, "You're going to have me here from now on. Trust me, I'll look after you."'

Bryan, of course, continued with Westlife, who were doing better than ever. In autumn 2002, reports emerged that the group had signed a new five-album deal worth £20 million, or £4 million each. And it was inevitable that sometimes Kerry missed that life, too. Asked if Bryan's being in a band had ever put pressure on the relationship, Kerry replied, 'It did when I first left Atomic Kitten, when I was pregnant. I'd given up my job, left my friends and family and moved to Ireland, where I didn't know anyone. I was so depressed I would sit around the house doing nothing and it drove me insane. With the girls, I was getting up at 4.30am and working until 2.30am the next day. I was desperate to get back out there working and I couldn't because I was pregnant.'

Perhaps because he now had a child of his own and another on the way, Bryan was also particularly sensitive now to the problems children faced, especially bullying. He and Mark made an emotional contribution to the *Daily*

Record's Save Our Kids campaign in Scotland, with Bryan talking about his own days being bullied at school. It was not only Kerry who had had the difficult background; Bryan had clearly had his own share of trauma, too.

'I was bullied throughout my childhood for being overweight, but in some ways it helped me, too,' he said. 'It hurt me a lot, especially as a youngster, but I eventually just got so used to being knocked. Because I got bullied so much, I actually worked on my self-confidence and somehow managed to build up my self-esteem. Rightly or wrongly, I learned to accept the bullying and it made me a better person in the long run.

'Even though it hurt, it was important for me to learn from it. I thought if I could try to get some control over the bullying, I could perhaps get through it. I don't know how I coped. I think I just got so used to being bullied I let it go. It almost became a part of my life. When people called me fat it would just bounce off me. It made me witty because I got used to firing quick, one-line answers back at people.'

It also, of course, made him tough. Just as Kerry learnt through early adversity how to fight for what she wanted in life, so Bryan did exactly the same. It was hardly any wonder they had come together as a couple; they had both had problems in childhood, followed by astonishing early success in their careers. Both could quite clearly relate to what the other was going through and, in the years they had together, established a very strong bond.

And perhaps it was the fact that he was to become a father for the second time that made Bryan start to question the way he was living his life. He found the lifestyle involved in being in a band exhausting and again admitted he had nearly left Westlife two years earlier. Indeed, given how difficult he had clearly found it, it was a wonder that he ended up staying with Westlife for as long as he did. Talking of leaving the band, he said, 'I used to feel like it when we had to work really hard. Now, because we're successful, it isn't as hard. Two years ago in America, just after we shot the Mariah Carey video, I cracked up and went home. It was all too much, a crazy schedule.

'We were travelling every day. We'd just come back from a gig in a football stadium in Indonesia, met the Royal Family and found out we had the biggest-selling album over there. We hopped on a plane to America, all buzzing. We arrived in New York to find there was no record company to meet us there. We had to get cabs from the airport, drag our luggage to the hotel and then two of us were sharing a room the size of a toilet.'

It was not, of course, the first time that Bryan had complained about that stint in the United States, but the memories plainly kept coming to the surface. It was the first sign of a dissatisfaction within him that was only going to grow. And he did display some sense of humour about it, recalling on one occasion how he had tried to be very rock 'n' roll by throwing a television out of the window, with a distinct lack of success. 'It just landed on top of me!' he said. 'I was a bit merry and I picked it up and fell backwards and woke up with the TV on my chest! It was a really bad time – I was stressed out, we'd been working for weeks and I hadn't seen Kerry or my family, then one of my friends got arrested for drink-driving. I just thought, "Aaargh!"'

But for now, at least, Bryan had Molly to console him while he worked. Now that Kerry was pregnant and easing off – slightly – on the workload, it was Bryan's turn to take their little girl around with him and they both loved it. Molly was entranced by the radio stations they visited, on one occasion putting on earphones and grabbing the microphone. 'It was great having her with me,' said an adoring Bryan. 'She loves being in the studio. She's a natural. Maybe she'll become a pop star when she grows up.' He was a doting father, taking every opportunity to lavish affection upon his little girl.

And with that, it was back on the road again, as the Westlife bandwagon roared off around Europe and the Far East. Bryan was clearly continuing to find it difficult, musing about when he and Kerry first met and, again, speculating that he would have fallen prone to drink and drug addiction if it hadn't been for her. Indeed, he offered an interesting insight into the time they were first together: 'The moment I saw her, I knew we would get married,' he said. 'When we first met, we had a fascination with each other. We were madly in love and it was very physical, if you know what I mean. The only way it has changed now is that I love her even more than when we got together. I've found out more about her and I like her even more.'

They were extremely touching words and, of course, Bryan now had Molly to think about, as well. He admitted it was hard being away from both his wife and his child. 'Molly started nursery today but I'm on the other side of the world,' he said sadly, in an interview at the time. 'That's hard, because I would have loved to have been there. She's my flesh and blood. I am so proud she is mine. I never imagined I would ever feel about anyone the way I feel about Molly. I always loved children, but it's different when you have one of your own. She wasn't planned, but she is the best surprise you could wish for. When she was born, I was numb. A couple of days later, the loving feeling kicked in and now every day she does something new. It's great.'

He was still noticeably dissatisfied, however. Westlife were even more successful than ever, and yet Bryan clearly wasn't enjoying it, continuing to brood about having to be apart from his family, and wondering what the future would bring. 'It is tough being away from my family so much, but I look at what I do now with one eye to the future,' he said. 'If Westlife carry on for ten more years, then great. But after that I will retire and stay home and wait for Molly to come home from school. Being away is made easier by the fact that I now have enough money to make sure she never wants for anything. If I wasn't in Westlife, I would probably be in college and not able to buy the things I can for her.'

Kerry felt the same and would often talk about the fact

that the two of them were working as hard as they could in order to establish financial security for their children. She, too, envisaged a future in which one day neither of them would have to work so hard. Kerry had lost none of her ability to be scathing, however. In the September before the new baby was born, David and Victoria Beckham announced the latest addition to their own family, a second son called Romeo. Kerry's feelings were soon known: 'I think any mother who names her baby Romeo must be having a laugh, and I feel that if it was up to me, she should be reported to the Social Services,' she snapped.

As for herself, she had decided to take a rest after her second child was born. 'I want to have at least two more children after this one, but I will take a break of a year or two after February when our second baby is due,' she said. 'After all, it's only my 22nd birthday this weekend and I'm not in that much of a rush. But I would like to have four children all together. For the moment, I am keeping myself busy between work and being pregnant.'

Indeed, her own career was continuing unabated. Kerry was by now appearing as one of the judges on *You're a Star*, an Irish television programme devised to find an act to represent Ireland in the Eurovision song contest. 'I don't know what sort of a judge I'll be,' said Kerry. 'I hope I'll be a nice one. My hormones will be all over the place, so I could be horrible! But we'll have a laugh. I hadn't met any of the other guys before. It's a perfect gig for me; I

Above: Mum Susan proudly shows off a photo of her daughter.

Below: Kerry with fellow Westlife wives, Gillian Filan, *left* and Georgina Byrne, *right*.

Kerry and Brian in
a Jordan car at the
British Grand Prix
at Silverstone

Above: A photocall before *I'm a Celebrity, Get Me Out of Here!* Kerry is pictured with fellow contestants Diane Modahl, Peter Andre, Jennie Bond, Mike Read, Neil 'Razor' Ruddock, Jordan, Alex Best, Lord Brocket and John Lydon.

Below left: An emotional Kerry is crowned Queen of the Jungle

Below right: Reunited with husband Brian after her time in the jungle.

Above: Kerry celebrates her success in the jungle with new friends Neil Ruddock and Jordan. Kerry and Jordan became such good friends that the glamour model asked Kerry to be bridesmaid at her wedding to Peter Andre.

Below: Having been homesick throughout *I'm a Celebrity…* Kerry was over the moon to be back with husband Brian and daughters Molly and Lilly Sue.

Above: Queen of the Jungle, Kerry, returns to her hometown of Warrington. She is met be crowds of adoring fans.

Below: Kerry is caught out by Ant and Dec in their 'Undercover Ant and Dec' feature in their hit show *Ant & Dec's Saturday Night Takeaway*.

Above: Keeping it in the family, Kerry, her mum Susan and daughter Molly.

Below: The former Atomic Kitten star turns her hand to TV presenting when she fronts the show *Britain's Sexiest...*

Above left: Kerry launches the award for the 'Best Fish and Chip Shop of the Year'.

Above right: Pictured starting the BUPA Great Manchester Run.

Below left: She was voted 'Celebrity Mum of the Year 2005'. This is the second time she has won the award.

Below right: Kerry with Dave Cunningham. She fell in love with her old friend foilowing the split from Brian, but the relationship wasn't to last.

Above left: Kerry with Mark Croft. She has put her past behind her and is looking to the future.

Above right: Kerry admitted that her pregnancy with Heidi Elizabeth took its toll. Here she is snapped running errands a few weeks before giving birth.

Middle: One of the first photos of mother and daughter.

Right: The new family home in an exclusive part of Wilmslow that Kerry hopes will be where she can create a happy family life with Mark and her girls.

want to stay in Ireland for the rest of the year and this isn't too strenuous.'

Even this programme, however, managed to carry with it a whiff of controversy. The judges were allowed a wild card, to send contestants on to the next round even if the public hadn't voted for them. Kerry chose to give her wild card to one Susan McFadden – Bryan's sister. She was accused in some quarters of blatant favouritism for obvious reasons, but her mother-in-law, Mairead, was quick to defend her daughter, saying that being Bryan's sister actually had considerable disadvantages.

'Susan is actually getting to the point now where she is not going to things any more because of people always putting her efforts down,' she said. As for Susan herself, it soon became apparent that she could actually sing, although the eventual winner of the show was Chris Doran, who went on to sing a song written by Bryan in the Eurovision Song Contest in Turkey that year.

Kerry herself was indignant at the claims. 'She's a fantastic singer, she's good–looking and just because she is my sister-in-law doesn't mean she can't follow her dream,' she said. 'It went against her that I was a judge. I put her through because she has a great talent. Just because she is Bryan's sister, people are against her, and I don't understand that.'

This controversy, however, was almost dwarfed by another remark she made on the show, when one of the contestants sang 'Whole Again', Atomic Kitten's biggest hit. 'It's a really hard song,' said Kerry. 'I couldn't sing it, that's why I only talk on the record.' She went on to repeat that on the Channel 4 show *The Salon*. 'I can't sing to save my life,' she announced. 'I never sang on any of the songs – I just spoke on them. You know that little verse on 'Whole Again' that was spoken? Very nicely done… I have to say, I'm a great speaker.' There was immediate and unexpected pandemonium and, despite later insisting she was only joking, it took Kerry some time to live that one down.

Kerry and Bryan also maintained their high profile as one of Dublin's première celebrity couples. Among many others, they were the star guests at the Rat Pack Ball, held at Dublin's Four Seasons Hotel, joining the likes of Michael Flatley and Sinead O'Connor. They were much talked about, as well. Kerry had very much settled into life in Dublin, now, and was completely at home with life in the Irish capital, just as she had been completely accepted in the circles in which she now mixed.

Christmas rolled round and, with it, a reunion for the family. Westlife still had a frantic schedule, but at least they were back in Britain, which gave Bryan more time to spend with Kerry and Molly. He was clearly pretty good with children generally, as Westlife spent time with young patients at the Royal Marsden cancer hospital in Sutton, chatting and signing autographs. Bryan went one better; he performed magic tricks, much to the delight of the children present. 'It's amazing to be able to come here and see the children's faces light up,' he said. 'They get really excited and it's nice to make them happy.' There was no question that he did that. Bryan was clearly quite committed to helping children when he had the power to do so.

The group generally were very good with their obligations towards young fans. Early in 2003, they again hosted the Childline concert. But Kerry and Bryan, of course, had their own offspring to deal with and had a bad scare in January that year when Molly suddenly became ill with a viral infection. Bryan cancelled an appearance with Westlife and the two rushed their child to hospital, where she was kept in overnight.

'Molly was a bit poorly, but she's fine now,' said a shaken Kerry afterwards. A source said, 'She was very ill on Thursday and they didn't have a clue what was wrong with her. They took her straight to hospital, where she was kept in overnight for tests. It turned out she had a really bad viral infection.' In the end, of course, she was fine, but given that Kerry was now only a month away from giving birth to the couple's second child, it was a nasty scare.

The other members of Westlife clearly adored Molly, too, and made a huge fuss of her when she was around. Some of them complained she made them feel broody. Kerry and Bryan watched all this with amusement, especially when Bryan confessed this sometimes led to a bit of confusion. 'When Molly sees a picture of me in a magazine, she points to it and says "Daddy", and we all go, "Aaaah,"' he said. 'But then she'll point to Mark and say "Daddy" and then Kian and say "Daddy" and on she goes right through the band. People often say to me it must be hard trying to juggle being a pop star with family life, but it can be just as hard, no matter what job you do. One of my best friends is about to get married. He works nine to five and has a child but I get to see more of Kerry and Molly than he does of his family.' But this was a rare moment of acceptance about the life he now led.

Bryan frequently spoke about the problems of life on the road, of missing his family and his home and of the general difficulty involved in being a pop star. When he finally did come to leave Westlife just over a year later, it was not that big a surprise to his fellow band members. He had been becoming increasingly disillusioned for a very long time.

Kerry wasn't really thrilled with the situation either, not least because of the long absences between the two. After all, she had given up her own pop career to raise a family and, although she understood the need for Bryan to work, she frequently wished that they could have been just a normal family. And as her pregnancy developed, it became harder than ever to sit at home, albeit with a successful television career now up and running, waiting for Bryan to come back from being on tour.

Delighted as she was with marriage and motherhood, it was a difficult life at times. 'I don't know how many times I used to say to Bryan, "Sometimes, I wish we had no money and just a nice little house,"' she said wistfully on one occasion. 'I would often cry and say, "Why can't you just work in McDonald's?"'

But, of course, he couldn't – neither of them could. Kerry remained as pleased and proud of her husband as ever and thrilled with her own success, but she was learning that there was a downside to celebrity – and this was it.

And, of course, the present was a contrast to the recent past; when she was in Atomic Kitten, Kerry had been in the thick of the action, whereas now, despite the fact that she was still working, she was of necessity slightly relegated to the sidelines. Having been so ambitious and having achieved so much, it didn't really suit her to stay at home so much of the time. Kerry was clearly keen to be out and about as quickly as she could.

Neither did she really enjoy being pregnant. It is a time when some women bloom, but Kerry didn't seem to be one of them; as she herself said, she always tended to end up unwell and feeling dreadful. 'I'm rubbish at being pregnant because I'm always poorly,' she said afterwards. 'I had a cyst before, when Molly was six months old, so I knew it was happening again when I was pregnant with Lilly.

'At first, the doctors thought it might be an ectopic pregnancy and we were rushed to hospital and I was frantically worried. When the doctors were talking to me about possible problems with the operation, I burst into tears and thought that if I lost the baby I'd try for another immediately, despite the fact that I hadn't wanted to be pregnant at the time. I was heartbroken and so was Bryan.

I was absolutely petrified but when they gave me a scan, they found it was a cyst. They operated immediately and removed it but they warned me that alone could make me lose the baby. I had to have loads of blood tests before they could give me the all-clear. I was in hospital for a week.' Mercifully, in the long run, everything was fine and Kerry gave birth to a happy and healthy baby, but the stress clearly took its toll.

Despite all that, the two were enormously looking forward to having a second child and even labour held no fears. Kerry revealed that after being given an epidural, she had slept through much of the first. 'I loved every minute of the birth,' she said. 'They actually woke me up to tell me it was time to push. I whispered, "Ssh, don't tell anyone. Just let me go back to sleep." Bryan was there holding my hand throughout and saying, "Don't worry, you're going to be a mum in a minute."'

When Molly finally arrived, Bryan the romantic exceeded himself, texting Kerry a poem he had written. 'That Friday arrived an angel from my heart,' it read. 'Her daddy's face, her mother's heart /A heart of gold to warm the place / I loved her mum so much before but now I love her even more.'

In February 2003, Kerry went into labour and gave birth to the couple's second daughter, Lilly Sue, at Mount Carmel Hospital in Dublin. Trooper that she was, she kept going with her work until the very last minute before her new daughter arrived. 'I worked all the way through [the pregnancy],' she said. 'I presented a show in Ireland called *You're a Star* on the Sunday night, then I went to bed, got up the next day and went straight into hospital to have Lilly.'

And now that, at long last, the baby had arrived, everyone was ecstatic. 'Mother and child are extremely happy and healthy,' said a spokesman for the couple. Bryan, as ever, could hardly contain himself. 'I'm absolutely over the moon,' he said. 'I feel delighted, it's another step closer to becoming a big family. We're all at Kerry's bedside today. I'd like to thank all of Westlife, too, for all their love and support.' And the band joined in the celebrations. Shane was named as Lilly's godfather, while there was more joshing about how the others all wanted babies now, too.

Indeed, with the new addition to their family, Kerry and Bryan seemed happier than ever. And, like so many parents, they found that having had one baby already, the second did not present quite as much of a challenge. Indeed, everything felt entirely natural. 'She's brilliant and I feel like she's been around for ever,' said an ecstatic Kerry.

'When I was in hospital, I felt anxious about going home with two kids, but now I think it's just perfect. People always say you never notice your second one and she's so good it's like she's not even here. I'm more relaxed with Lilly, because Molly's at the age where I'm having to run after her. I'm absolutely in love with the girls, but it's dead weird to think that we're only 22 and we've got two children.'

And, of course, neither was planned – not that that mattered at all to the proud parents, who, in actual fact, appeared not to be able to get over their luck. 'Neither Lilly nor Molly were planned,' Kerry confirmed. 'While Bryan was away, I did seven pregnancy tests and I couldn't believe they were all positive! I just thought, not again! I started crying because I couldn't believe it. Molly was not even one and I was just getting back to work.'

There were signs, though, that Bryan was thinking of other matters, too. Along with his family, his own future was uppermost in his thoughts. At around the time of Lilly's arrival, he joined up with the Irish band Fifth Avenue for an impromptu song at the Childline concert, after which there were rumours that he would actually become their manager. He had been writing songs for other artists, too, and was clearly beginning to think of a future beyond Westlife. And although he remained committed to his family, for the very first time there were indications that, well, he was awfully young for the role he was now playing.

Westlife announced plans for another tour and Bryan, rather surprisingly, given how he had talked about touring in the past, seemed delighted – not least because it would give him the chance to relax. 'I'm looking forward to hitting the road,' he said. 'I do my share of diapers and it's hard, tiring work. I can hardly believe I'm going through all that again. I haven't been getting much sleep, but the tour will be much more relaxing and gives me a chance to rest.'

But he remained keen to emphasise the fact that he was a family man now, and knew where his duties lay. 'I see my children and know I have responsibilities,' he said. 'I had to grow up. Lilly cries a lot more than Molly ever did and is quite a different baby. But Molly is very affectionate and protective of her and doesn't get jealous. Being a dad again makes life much more worthwhile and I'm loving it. From being single to married, then a dad to family man, there have been a lot of big life changes in the last couple of years. But I handled them well.'

The very fact he was thinking along those lines, however, was a clear indication that he was thinking quite deeply now about the future route his life should take. But for now, all was well. Both Kerry and Bryan were enjoying parenthood and enjoying their careers. Indeed, for both, considerable triumphs lay ahead.

10

FILLING ROLES

Kerry and Bryan were settled and fulfilled but, of course, two very small children were extremely hard work. Both sets of parents pitched in to provide what assistance they could, but there was still an awful lot for Kerry and Bryan to do, so much so that they also took on people to assist them in looking after the children, especially as Kerry began accepting more work commitments. Indeed, in Kerry's case, it was a necessity, to say nothing of the fact that the two of them also wanted at least a little time to themselves.

'We have lots of help from our families,' Kerry explained. 'Bryan's mum gave up her job to help look after Molly, so any time we wanted to go out, such as Valentine's Day, we could. It's important to have time for your relationship, otherwise you drift apart. We've got a nanny now because it wouldn't be fair on Bryan's mum to look after two children – she's got her own life. I need a nanny because I travel so much and airlines won't let you travel on your own with two kids under two.'

And despite the fact that Kerry and Bryan obviously doted on their children, people continued to ask them about their age. It was hard to believe that they were both so young; married, with two children and very successful careers on either side, both had already experienced more than many people decades older had done. By today's standards, of course, the two were very young to have started a family, but Kerry was quite clearly irritated whenever the was question raised. She and Bryan were besotted with the children, and both had taken extremely well to parenthood, with both doing their share.

'If you went back twenty years when my mum was my age, people were getting married at sixteen and no one said there was anything wrong with it,' she said. 'Now women wait until they're forty to get married and have kids, but who's to say who is right or wrong? If we weren't famous and didn't have the money, it would probably be the last thing on our mind, but we've been around the world and done so much at a young age.'

She was right about that life experience, but what she didn't perhaps realise was that she was also very mature for her age – or rather, that she was more mature than most people would have been in their early twenties and thus more able to handle increased responsibilities. Much is made of the fact that Kerry can be as loud and brash as the best of them, but the fact remains that she had to deal with very difficult experiences in her childhood, and this was bound to have left its mark.

She and her own mother were as close as two peas in a pod, but even so, Kerry had sometimes had to assume the role of carer when she was still a child, something that was bound to enable her to handle the role of being a wife and mother much younger than many of her contemporaries would have been able to do. It also, as she herself realised, gave her a yearning for security and a settled family life.

And she admitted that her childhood continued to haunt her – perhaps even more now that she was a mother herself. She was constantly aware of the difference between the past and the present and would speak openly about the trauma she had endured when she was a girl. 'I find it really hard to let go of the past and I dwell on it a lot,' she said. 'People think I've got everything, but they don't understand how hard I've had to work. I'm so happy that I got married young and have two kids I love, and my background's made me stronger.

'You're given two paths in life, the right one and the wrong one, and which way you choose depends on what kind of person you are. I could be on drugs, an alcoholic and a thief, but decided against that. One of the reasons I pushed myself was that I was in Care at school and I was immediately perceived as trouble through no fault of my own.' She had, however, used the experience to make her more resilient, a quality that has appeared over and over throughout her life, and that was to stand her in very good stead in the future.

As the world now knew, Kerry had come through problems both in the past and more recently and, now that she was feeling more settled, she was more able to discuss what she went through when the incident concerning Bryan and the lap dancer came out. It emerged that poor Kerry had taken it much more badly than she had ever let on at the time, actually having had to be tranquillised when she heard the news. 'The shock was literally as if someone had hit me in the stomach,' she said. 'I dropped the phone and I remember my mum holding me down while his mum shoved two Valium tablets in my mouth. I even took my wedding ring off.

'I couldn't get hold of Bryan, so I rang my aunt. She read the newspaper to me over the phone and I was screaming and crying. I thought, "I can't believe this." I rang Bryan back and he wouldn't answer, no one would. I called his manager Louis Walsh and screamed at him, but he didn't have a clue. I called Shane, Kian, everyone that came to mind. I was screaming down the phone, "You arseholes. You knew all about this and didn't tell me. You let me walk down that aisle like an idiot." I went ballistic.'

It had been a terrible trauma and, if truth be told, the hurt had never totally gone away. And, of course, the betrayal was all the harder to bear, given that Bryan, more than anyone, knew how Kerry had suffered when she was growing up – and the fact that although she found it hard to trust people generally, she did trust him.

The papers had originally claimed that Bryan had slept with the lap-dancer; by now, it was clear that what had actually happened was that she had performed oral sex. Kerry recalled with horror the moment she found out the truth. 'He admitted a sex act had taken place during a lap-dance, but nothing more,' she said. 'I just collapsed on the floor, shouting, "No, my Bryan wouldn't do that to me." He knew all about the shit I went through growing up. He knew about the foster carers, the eight schools I'd been to. He knew I'd been through a lot of crap in my life. That's why it was so hard to accept.'

As for Bryan himself, he was more ashamed of what had happened than ever. He realised just how badly his actions had affected his wife, on top of which the lap-dancer involved was simply refusing to go away, threatening to sue Bryan unless he admitted what had happened. It increased the stress on him enormously, while making matters even worse for Kerry. He was also worried about what the claims that he had taken drugs that night would do to his image, and was anxious to play that aspect of the story down.

'I feared Kerry would believe the whole story in the paper,' he said. 'I felt suicidal and wanted to die. There's no life for me without Kerry. I'm big enough to say that I've managed to make some stupid mistakes. Sure, I allowed Amy Barker to give me oral sex on my stag night, I've made that clear in the past. However, I did not take cocaine.'

Life did, however, have to go on. Bryan was continuing to develop a career outside Westlife, possibly with a view towards an eventual solo career. His songwriting talents were coming on strongly; he had written 'A Better Plan' for Simon Casey on *You're a Star*, and had also written a track for Louis Walsh's latest find, Girls Aloud. But the pressures of work didn't let up. Rumours were circulating that Kerry had been reduced to tears when she asked him to spend more time at home with her and the children, something he implicitly accepted was true.

'That's something that happens and it's going to happen until Westlife is over,' he said. 'Westlife isn't going to last for ever. In ten years time, we'll only be in our early 30s and we can retire and sit at home. I know what me and Kerry are like… if I left Westlife tomorrow and came home, in two weeks she'd want me to go back to work and I'd want to go back to work.' These were the pressures that affected any couple with high-powered careers, but Kerry and Bryan had not yet managed to find the happy medium that suited them both.

Indeed, this was a stressful time for Bryan in other ways, as well. He failed to pull over when the police saw him speeding away from a Belfast concert in his yellow Ferrari Spider Modena 360. Luckily for him, he was only given an official warning when the police arrived at his hotel. 'All the lads like to drive themselves home whenever they can,' said a source close to the group. 'Bryan was with one of his minders in the Ferrari and decided to see what the car could do. At some point, he raced past a police car and through a red light. The cops tried to pull him over but he didn't see them. He just didn't know they were trying to pull him over. He got the fright of his life when he was told the police were waiting for him in reception. They gave him a right telling off and he apologised.' In fairness to Bryan, he had been trying to escape hordes of screaming fans, something the police did take account of. Over-eager fans were not a one-off, either; they continued to smuggle themselves into hotels and cupboards in order to meet their idols, creating, among other things, a security risk.

Bryan's troubles didn't end there. He had still not sold his home in County Wicklow, and had now had to reduce the asking price to just £700,000. However, life perked up when, like his wife, he won a Parent of the Year competition, in his case to be named Britain's Dad of the Year, coming in ahead of Tony Blair and David Beckham. And Westlife continued to be massively popular, with the boys performing to sell-out crowds wherever they went. And while life was difficult, it had its rewards. It was, after all, a Ferrari, not an old Vauxhall, that he was driving when stopped by the police.

Bryan was not alone in pursuing his career. As she settled down to looking after the two girls, Kerry had also found another outlet on television – the lunchtime show *Loose Women*, made by Granada. The show had originally begun in 1999 and, as the name suggested, consisted of four women chatting about issues of the day.

Kerry was delighted with the new development, not least

because she saw it as a way, once and for all, of establishing her own identity, rather than by being identified by who she was married to or the band to which she had once belonged. 'It wasn't the Westlife tag I wanted to get away from, but the fact that I'm always being known as once being in Atomic Kitten,' she explained. 'Don't get me wrong, I'm very proud of being in the band, but it's been three years now and it'd be nice to be known as Kerry McFadden.'

Kerry was a natural on the show. Some people commented that she could seem loud-mouthed, but this, after all, was what the programme-makers wanted; a wallflower would not have provided much in the way of entertainment. And as ever, where Kerry was concerned, controversy was never far away, in this case about the weight she'd lost after having Lilly Sue. Kerry rather recklessly mentioned that she had used slimming tablets on air; as ever, a mini furore erupted. 'I've managed to lose half-a-stone in a perfectly healthy way,' said a slightly weary Kerry after the issue had calmed down. 'We were talking on *Loose Women* about me taking slimming pills.

'But the truth was, I was in a chemist and I bought some herbal slimming tablets. I thought I'd try them to see what they were like. I only remembered to take two because I'm terrible when it comes to taking pills, hence the two babies. I don't think they even work, to be honest. I lost half-a-stone purely from running around after the kids and, as for eating, I've got into a healthy routine of making sure I eat breakfast and having smaller meals – and I've also been going to the gym.' This was a change from previous habits – Kerry's favourite foods had always included chips but, especially in the wake of having two children, she was aware that a career in showbusiness means staying in shape.

Given the fact that both were doing well professionally, however, the perennial problem of too little time to spend together continued to be an issue for Kerry and Bryan. They continued to talk about it publicly, a sign that it really was a problem that had not yet been resolved. 'It is hard, I suppose, because when we're not working, we're looking after the kids,' said Bryan. 'We get so little time off and, because of this, we feel it would be unfair to offload the kids on to one of our mothers so we can spend time together.'

'We do love to go out, though. If we're in Dublin, we love to go to Lillie's Bordello and we also go to a karaoke bar nearer home. We always get up and sing and nobody bothers us. At the start of the evening, we have no intention of singing, then we go and get drunk and you can't get us off the stage.' The two were also talking about having more children and perhaps even adopting, although both agreed the time was not right at the moment. Bryan, incidentally, was as keen to adopt as Kerry and for exactly the same reason, that Kerry's deprived background had given both the desire to offer help to a child.

Westlife were certainly busy. One minute they were appearing in Hong Kong, the next topping the bill along-side Luciano Pavarotti at a Royal Variety Performance, where other performers included Busted, Daniel Bedingfield and Donny Osmond. The show was to be presented by Cat Deeley. A new album, *Turn Around*, was due out at the end of the year and, again, they were performing at a Children in Need concert. Other performers at Belfast's Odyssey Arena included Simply Red and Girls Aloud. The boys were busier than ever.

They were also, especially Bryan, increasingly aware of their appearance. There had been hints from both their management and their peers in the industry that they should all, especially Bryan, start showing a little more concern about their physiques, and Bryan, for one, was finally heeding the advice. He had become a devotee of the Atkins diet and was indeed losing weight. 'It's the best thing ever… I've lost a stone in two weeks,' he said. 'I can have a big fry-up with loads of sausages and rashers of bacon in the morning and a Burger King in the evenings – just without the bread. It's great.' And with that, the boys were off on their first ever visit to India, where they had amassed a massive following.

Not that Kerry was exactly being idle at the time. As well as her television work, she was trying out some stage appearances, most notably at the risqué *Vagina Monologues* at the Palace Theatre, Manchester. She was appearing alongside the actress Jan Shepherd and Ellen Thomas, who played the secretary Liz in *Teachers*, and received rave reviews.

'The *Vagina* interviews were conducted with women of all ages, ethnicity, religion and background and are a funny and yet moving collection of stories at times hilarious, at times poignant,' said one review. 'I think Kerry just about pulled it off – she was clearly nervous but settled down and, in the end, gave a very creditable performance.'

She was certainly in very good company. The theatrical experience – it couldn't really be called a play – was devised by Eve Ensler and since then has gone on to be performed by some of the most famous women in the world, among them Glenn Close, Kate Winslet, Whoopi Goldberg, Calista Flockhart and Jerry Hall. She was trying out her acting in another way, too, appearing in an 'undercover' sketch on *Saturday Night Takeaway*, before going on to present the *Toy of the Year Show* with Eamonn Holmes – actually a phone-in, in which 100 of the most popular toys were featured across 10 categories. Her television experience was increasing by the day.

But her greatest challenge was still to come. Kerry was already a famous woman in the world of showbusiness, but she was about to embark on a challenge that would make her a household name. Kerry, who claimed to have a fear of heights and insects, who hated being away from her family and who had once talked about her loathing of spiders, was about to make her bravest move yet. Along with a host of other celebrities… she was jungle-bound.

11

JUNGLE BELLES

It had become a phenomena in television circles. *I'm a Celebrity ... Get Me Out of Here!* had started several years earlier to generally low expectations and had become one of the most popular and gripping television programmes around. More than that, the people it attracted to take part were actually genuine celebrities, and with each series that passed, the higher up the pecking order the celebrities were.

This was due to a paradox: that the people who took part discovered that, stripped of make-up, subjected to hardship and forced to endure gruesome trials, they actually became more, rather than less, sympathetic to the public at large, encouraging genuinely famous people to take part. And, in some cases, the show had had a rejuvenating effect on people's careers. After Tony Blackburn won the first series, many people had become much more aware of just how lucrative a stint in the jungle could be.

The general format of the show was simple – presided over by the ubiquitous Ant and Dec, whom Kerry had already worked with on other programmes, a group of celebrities were dumped in a remote part of the Australian jungle (actually, it wasn't that remote, according to some people) they were deprived of food and then made to undergo horrible ordeals, called Bushtucker Trials, to be able to win some provisions. The longer they suffered, the more food they got. Viewers back in the UK were able to vote on which celeb had to endure which trial, and it was also the viewers who voted the contestants off. It was simple and incredibly popular television.

Rumours had been doing the rounds for some time that Kerry was to take part in the series beginning in January 2004. Bryan was said to be a little worried about her taking part, particularly at what she might say about their relationship – although given how much both had opened their hearts over the previous year, it was difficult to see what more could be said – but in the fullness of time, the rumours turned out to be absolutely correct. Kerry was indeed going to take part.

At first, there was some surprise at the news. Although Kerry's background in Care was no secret, it was not widely understood quite how tough circumstances had forced her to become; she was still widely seen to be a fluffy blonde, and while she was actually nothing of the sort, that inner steel was not yet known. Kerry did nothing to dispel that initial perception of her, either, talking brightly about what life would be like with her new group of adventurous friends. 'I'm used to pulling my weight... living with Bryan, you have to!' she said. 'In the camp, I won't mind cleaning up, it won't bother me. I don't want to be the lazy one in there. I will try my best to get away with it, though.'

One downside was that she was going to have to miss Lilly Sue's first birthday, and that clearly made Kerry feel a bit down. 'I'm going to miss my kids the most, my TV, mobile phone... oh, and Bryan!' she said. 'He's going to be looking after the kids; I'm really going to miss him because we haven't gone a day since we've been together when we haven't spoken on the phone when he's away or I'm away, so that's going to be hard. It's going to be torture. I'm going to miss TV, especially *Friends*. I don't actually watch that much TV as I'm either working or changing nappies. I probably will even miss changing nappies; I won't miss changing Bryan's, though!'

But she was under no illusions as to what it would entail. There had been enough scenes of celebrities balancing on high wires, swimming with sharks and eating goodness knows what for everyone in the country to know that appearing in *I'm a Celebrity...* was not an easy ride, and Kerry was well aware she would be put to the test. Nevertheless, she was prepared to go ahead. 'I'm one of these kinds of people who like to say I've been there and done it, I really want the experience,' she said. 'I don't want to think, "Oh, I wish I'd gone now." I've been offered it and… why not? And I'm going to raise so much money for charity, the longer they keep me in there, the more I make.'

As to what the actual mechanics of the camp would be, Kerry had decided on her approach. 'Depending what the situation is in camp, I might speak my mind,' she said. 'I don't want to hurt anybody's feelings, but if someone's going to have a go at me or something, I'm not going to sit there and keep my gob shut. Of course, I'm worried about how the viewers will perceive me, I think everybody is. I don't want anyone thinking I'm a stuck-up cow or anything, which I'm not.

'I'm a really down-to-earth person, funny, I like a good laugh, I'm up for anything, I'll try anything once if it's within reason… I'm most worried that people don't like me or if I don't get on with the other celebrities. I remember watching it and they tend to go off in two groups and say bad things about each other, so I don't want people to say bad things about me behind my back. I get on with alcoholic party animals best! I've only seen bits and pieces… I scared myself seeing what they had to do. Phil Tufnell was my favourite last year. I saw Danniella have her breakdown and I guess I can understand. You never know, I might break down, so I'll just have to wait and see what happens.'

She was certainly being brave. 'I'm absolutely petrified of everything and anything… I haven't got a clue how I'm going to deal with that… I'll probably end up having a nervous breakdown,' she said. 'I'll probably end up screaming. I'm petrified of heights, more than spiders or anything. Snakes don't bother me too much, but I wouldn't want one in my bed.'

As for the other great challenge – going without make-up for the duration – Kerry was more relaxed. 'I don't mind having the cameras around… when Danniella was on *Loose Women*, she said that you totally forget the cameras are there. It won't bother me at all. Not having make-up doesn't bother me; I don't really wear it unless I'm working anyway. I never really look at myself as a celebrity, but what I'd miss most about celebrity life would have to be Chinese takeaways… I love my takeaways!'

Kerry, as was to be expected, was actually becoming excited about going into the jungle and her enthusiasm spilled over. 'The most adventurous thing I've done is crazy golf!' she said. 'The most crazy thing I've done is probably jet ski-ing or going on a banana boat or something. This is a really big experience for me, I'll probably be the first one to say, "Get me out of here!" I can drink anybody under the table! And I have been watching *Castaway* so I've been getting tips from Tom Hanks.'

This cheery attitude was only to be expected from the very chirpy Kerry, but it concealed more nerves than she initially let on. Indeed, she became so wound up about the ordeal that lay ahead that she actually had to go to hospital after becoming severely stressed while visiting her mother Sue. 'We were supposed to go out to the pub, but I threw up as soon as I got to my mum's,' she said. 'They ended up rushing me to hospital with severe stomach pains and I was there for a day-and-a-half. I made myself ill because I was so worried about leaving Bryan and my girls. My worst fear is that the British public will see me on TV and hate me.' Thankfully, it was a fear that was not to be realised.

It was also reported that she gave Bryan a rather touching goodbye present before going into the jungle – a Trabant, the rather down-at-heel German car made famous by Bono. Bryan was delighted. 'They have all the money in the world, so getting a flash car for Bryan wasn't a problem for Kerry,' said a friend. 'But she wanted something different – something Bryan could have a laugh in. So she came up with the idea of the Trabant. I'm not sure how much it cost but he absolutely loves it. Bryan is a bit of a rebel underneath it all and he does things his own way. So driving around in one of these cars when he could have been swanning around in a Ferrari or a Porsche gives him a real buzz.'

Kerry recovered from her nerves in time to fly to Australia, where she met the other nine contestants competing in the show. They were the glamour model Jordan, Alex Best, the beautiful wife (at the time) of the footballer George Best, the pop star Peter Andre and Lord Brocket, an aristocrat who had been jailed for a false insurance claim, and who was by now becoming something of a minor celebrity. In addition, there was the soccer star Neil Ruddock, the royal reporter Jennie Bond, DJ Mike Read, the ex-Olympic athlete Diane Modahl and, the contestant who probably attracted most publicity, John Lydon, who had once been Johnny Rotten in the Sex Pistols. It was a very diverse group.

As the contestants prepared to enter the jungle, the programme's publicity machine swung into action. Much was made of a tropical storm that played havoc with the campsite just before the celebrities were due to go in, with some gleeful predictions that the ensuing mud would bring any number of nasties to the surface. Amid great fanfare, it was announced that the celebrities involved had all signed disclaimers clearing the programme-makers of responsibility should any of them die a horrible, jungle-related death, although what chance the producers stood of attracting future celebrities in such an eventuality was not mentioned. 'The possibility of deadly snakes and poisonous spiders creeping into the jungle camp is very real,' one onlooker warned. 'The show's bosses have taken it so seriously, they have experts and snake-handlers on hand. The stars have all been fully briefed on what to do if it does happen.'

Bravely putting the incredible danger behind them, the celebrities revealed what individual luxuries they would be taking into the camp – Kerry chose a photograph of Bryan, Molly and Lillie Sue. John Lyndon rather mysteriously opted for a pot of Vaseline, Lord Brocket for axle grease (to stop creepy crawlies from climbing up him) and Peter Andre took his lucky black bandana. Alex Best and Jennie Bond both opted for items to help with their appearance, a pair of tweezers for the former and a lipstick for the latter. Jordon wanted a hot water bottle, Diane Modahl a pair of trainers, Mike Reid a pen and paper and Neil Ruddock, who had initially been tipped by bookies to win the show, a rubber ring.

And so the ordeal began. Kerry almost immediately displayed remarkable prescience by informing Jordan that she had an admirer in the form of Peter Andre, while Jordan enthralled viewers when she appeared to finish with her boyfriend Scott on live television because he hadn't wished her luck. This did not save her, alongside Neil, from the first challenge, in which both had to wear see-through helmets, which were then filled with bugs, snakes and spiders. John was next up for a Bushtucker Trial, when he was sent into battle with some nasty-looking ostriches, a challenge he greeted by announcing, 'I'm dying to do something.'

In the event, John, who was covered in treacle and had bird seed spread on his protective clothing, got six meals out of a possible ten after the twelve birds, whom he referred to as 'fat budgies,' managed to knock his goggles off. Indeed, he was very good humoured about his trial, especially when he discovered where the eggs he was expected to find were. 'Did you have to bury them so deep?' he demanded. 'I've never known such spite! They are ground in. What a death trap! What a set-up! It's fantastic!'

In this early stage of the show, there was a good deal of speculation that Kerry might actually quit. She and Mike Reid were sent to collect a celebrity chest, and while

Mike happily abseiled down a waterfall, Kerry had an attack of nerves and wanted to go back. Afterwards, she was annoyed with herself. 'I went all dizzy and my chest closed,' she said. 'I thought I'd been bitten by a spider but it was just me having a panic attack again. I sat down with the doctor and had a cry. I don't want to let everyone down. I've let myself down.' Neither was she cheered to discover that the cause of the problem, the celebrity chest, contained only two miniature bottles of port and a cigar. 'That's crap,' she said.

Matters didn't really seem to improve when Kerry was picked for the next Bushtucker Trial, not least because she burst into tears when told she was picked. The trial wasn't much fun, either – Kerry was put in a Perspex box full of eels, spiders and leeches, which was submerged into the lake beneath it in three minutes. In that time, Kerry had to fit ten keys into ten matching locks. In the event, she only managed two, to get two stars. 'I've done really crap,' she said gloomily afterwards. 'I got two. I'm giving up smoking. That's really abysmal, isn't it? I'm really disappointed with two stars for everyone.'

Kerry was, however, beginning to demonstrate a flair for attracting people's attention. Earlier in the show, she had been chatting to Peter, whose attraction to Jordan was becoming increasingly obvious. 'You can see you're physically attracted to her,' said Kerry. 'You definitely want a piece of cake, you do. Come on, be a man and admit it. Who wouldn't? Kate's [Jordan's real name] a woman. All women play. You're only human. Fucking hell, I'm female and I want a piece of her.' That remark, unsurprisingly, was widely reported throughout the press.

Publicity aside, however, her constant tearfulness and seeming inability to cope had even her nearest and dearest concerned about her wellbeing. Kerry's mother Sue, who had been watching the programme from her home in Warrington, was quite clearly distressed at what she was seeing on the screen. 'It's heartbreaking to see Kerry struggle to cope in the jungle,' she said.

'I have cried all night. She is going through agony but I am helpless to do anything about it. I hate watching her get upset. It kills me. And it has been torture watching her get worse and worse. She isn't enjoying herself and said she might only last a couple of days in the camp. She's been unwell ever since she got to Australia. It has had a drastic effect on her personality. I think she's going to crack up. Winning a show is not worth having such a horrible time. There's no shame in saying, "Get me out of here."'

Bryan was equally concerned, although in his case he was keen for his wife to continue. Max Clifford, who was handling PR for the couple, said, 'Bryan is watching things very carefully and he's worried about Kerry.' Bryan himself, meanwhile, sent Kerry a text message: 'come on kez, do it for me babe! Luv u, bryan xx.'

Kerry began to cheer up. She remained a confidante of Peter, who was clearly increasingly smitten with Jordan, and, on the day wine was sent in to celebrate Alex's birthday, was forced to tell Charlie Brocket off for unhooking her bra – three times.

This year's mix was proving to be a potent one. Quite a few of the contestants were calling attention to themselves in one way or another, with Jordan in particular creating various dramas. Apart from the growing flirtation with Peter, she was also both coming under fire from John and darkly hinting about secrets to be included in her forthcoming autobiography, *Being Jordan*. 'If someone upsets me, I believe you can get them back one way or another,' she murmured ominously, before whispering something to her little circle that she refused to divulge to the public as a whole. 'We'll see who has a smile on their face. I was saying stuff about my book… just little hints… It's a scandal around a football thing. Believe me, it's a scandal. I always come up with surprises, me.'

Meanwhile, John was doing a very good impression of a grouchy old man, fulminating against Jordan for what he perceived as idleness. 'I just don't like lazy people,' he announced after taking part in a Mad Hatter's Tea Party, complete with tea and cucumber sandwiches, held in honour of his birthday. 'I don't like carrying dead weight. I don't. That's coming across now really, really strongly. It's a good-for-nothing waste of time at the moment. Make her get up and do something. Give her a poke up the arse like she deserves. It's not right, she's dragging it all down to silliness. Much more of that and I'm walking, I'm telling you. I'm not here to support that kind of crap. I'm here to have a laugh with some good people. She can't even bloody wash a tea cup without the effort of it all. And it eats and it's non-stop and it don't cook bugger all.' He was clearly a little upset.

But the others were having far too much fun to worry. Charlie Brocket managed to overcome his fear of heights to tackle the Ladder Lottery, during which he had to collect flags from rope ladders suspended above the jungle floor; while Kerry, Jordan, Alex and Peter got together for a group massage session. Then came the greatest test of all for Kerry and, indeed, Jordan – they were told that they were up next for a Bushtucker Trial, which in this case was going to be eating insects. Kerry was not thrilled; she covered her mouth and started to shake, although in the event the girls did well. Alex was the next to do a trial, enduring eels, cockroaches and chicken feathers to get the meals. Charlie Brocket generously helped her to wash down afterwards.

As Kerry began to relax a little more, she also began to open up about her past. It emerged that in the days she was in Atomic Kitten, she had collapsed, something she was only able to deal with with the help of Bryan. 'Before we got married or had kids, I had a nervous breakdown,' she told Diane. 'I had a lot of trouble. We were in dance rehearsals and I locked myself in the toilet and I couldn't come out and I was uncontrollable and I couldn't think and I was screaming. And Bryan was doing a TV show somewhere. He got a phone call and he left the studio, against all the other people saying, "Don't go, you've got to work," got a car, stormed in, kicked the toilet door in and said, "This girl's not well, I'm taking her home."

'He's my hero. He's there to look after me and I just love that. I've never had a dad. I've never met him and looking at him as a dad to my kids, that just melts my heart, I just love it.' Coincidentally, at around the time Kerry was confiding this, the news broke that Atomic Kitten were to split up, something that left her looking astonished. 'I can't believe they've split,' she said.

The first evacuee from the camp was Mike Reid, who was clearly not pleased by the turn of events. He had been a relatively quiet presence on the show and now felt that the producers had been far too keen on the antics of Jordan, Brocket and Co, to the detriment of the others. 'It's a farce,' he was heard to say as he left the set. 'I didn't realise until I'd left but they cut everything out except the salacious bits. I couldn't go around touching the girls and undoing their bra straps. It's not what I do.'

Mike also revealed what it was that Jordan had told the others; namely, that she had had an affair with David Beckham. The Beckham's lawyers promptly threatened to sue, but Mike Reid put his finger on the button when he pointed out what Jordan's real reason for making that claim was. 'By saying that sort of thing on the show, you know you'll wipe all the other headlines out,' he said.

The antics in the jungle rumbled on. Along with Charlie, Kerry was sent to collect a celebrity chest from the treetops; this one was much more worthwhile than the one she had got before in that it had enough coffee, whiskey and cream to make Irish coffees for everyone. There was, however, a small spat with the good Lord B, who returned to the camp carrying the chest alone. 'I thought there was no "I" in team,' snapped Kerry. 'I thought it was supposed to be a team effort, but every suggestion I made was wrong. I don't like his game – the game he is playing. I refuse to get involved in it. He left me stood up there like a wanker. I like Charlie, but I'm not getting involved in this bitchiness that he's doing.'

More publicity was generated by claims that none other than the Queen was watching the programme, while Jordan and Peter's will-they-won't-they behaviour kept everyone glued to the screen. Meanwhile, Jordan's boyfriend – or rather, as he had discovered along with the rest of the world, now ex–boyfriend – was not amused by events. He flew to Australia to rescue the relationship, a task in which he sadly failed.

Neil Ruddock was the next to be evicted, after which John decided to seize the initiative. He carried out his threat and stormed out of the camp. It had all been too much, especially Jordan. 'These are daft, lazy and crazy people,' he said. As for Jordan, 'That's Silicon Valley, the crap end of it. That's one really lazy, spoilt sod. Who raises these people? I live in a very different world; no disrespect to this game, but I play a bigger one – or a smaller one.'

Back in the camp itself, Lord Brocket was also busy stirring, describing Jennie Bond to Jordan as an 'old slag' who was 'dogmatic' and 'arrogant'. Indeed, a real feud had now started to develop between Jennie and Charlie, not least because the latter sensed a certain chippiness from the former. Jennie seemed to offend Lord B greatly when she referred to his 'moneyed background'. 'Three times you have killed a conversation by saying I am from a rich class or moneyed background, when neither money nor background has anything to do with the conversation,' he said irritably. Jennie looked bemused. 'What a strange offence,' she said.

But that wasn't all. Earlier, when Jennie set off for a Bushtucker Trial, Charlie said venomously, 'Maybe the ratbag will drown. I don't like her at all. The main problem is that she's just very false about everything… she's seriously false.' Indeed, he moaned on to Alex, 'It's so fake. In prison, we used to weed them out in seconds, people who used to put on an act or a show or be something that everyone knew they weren't, a sort of Hannibal thing, you detect it very quickly.' There was clearly no love lost between the two.

But Brocket's bitchiness, entertaining as it might have been for the viewers, had a most unexpected side-effect. Until he stalked out, John had been favourite to win the show, with viewers then switching their allegiance to Lord Brocket. But his sniping about Jennie completely turned the audience against him, with one major beneficiary – Kerry. Previously, when she had kept breaking down, such a result would have been almost inconceivable – and yet she was now being spoken of as a potential winner, the first woman ever to be so. John, for a start, wanted her to win. 'I'd like her to do it for her kids,' he said. 'She's a tough little cookie underneath all that. I think it would be great for her – she deserves it. She's a real person.'

It was an astonishing turn of events. Ladbrokes confirmed what had happened, slashing odds on her winning from 2-1 to 4-5. 'Punters are smitten with the former Atomic Kitten,' said Warren Lush, a spokesman for the company. 'While her former bandmates have split up and their stardom is fading, Kerry is on the up and is odds-on favourite to become the very first Queen of the Jungle. Viewers are attracted to the fact that she appears to be a normal, down-to-earth girl. Lord Brocket's fortunes have changed dramatically in the last twenty-four hours. He was hot favourite to win after John Lydon left but his odds drifted when he revealed his bitchiness and contempt for Jennie Bond. This could prove to be his downfall.'

They were right. Jordan had already been evicted, and Charlie B was next to go, having further commented about Jennie Bond that she 'should be recycled into something useful'. Jennie responded by putting his pink tutu – it had been worn amid all the fun of the show – on a bonfire. Before he left, however, there was a riotous evening, in which Kerry managed to get extremely drunk. She had been feasting on beer, wine and champagne and clearly needed help from the others; after being escorted to bed, she called, 'Oh no, I'm really drunk, Jennie. Champagne and beer don't go.'

'They probably don't,' said Jennie as she helped her to the loo, 'but we'll be all right.'

Kerry was still not quite herself. She next found herself opening the door to visit the Bush Telegraph, the private diary room, where she screamed in fright on spotting something nasty. 'I'm not coming into there until you get rid of that fucking thing!' she cried. 'Get rid of it or else I'm not coming in.'

Lord Brocket came pounding to the rescue and got rid of the offending insect. 'There was a petrified little cricket trying to get out and she thought it was a praying mantis,' he explained. 'After a couple of glasses of champagne, she thought it was out to get her. The poor thing was petrified and I shooed it out and she screamed because it was coming towards her.' Kerry eventually felt better.

She was also thrilled about the prospect of seeing Bryan again. 'Fourteen days – two weeks – I haven't spoken to my husband,' she said. 'Never again. I get excited thinking about seeing him again. And that nervous feeling… like on your first date. I remember when I was pregnant with Lilly, Bryan phoned up and I was really down in the dumps. He said, "I've got a babysitter. I've booked a room at the Four Seasons and I'm coming to pick you up. I want you to be ready." I was all excited. It was like a first date. He knocked on the door all dressed up, and he stood there with a red rose. I love him that much. I could cry with my love for him.'

'That's nice,' said a very sympathetic Jennie. 'I hope it lasts for another forty years, fifty years, sixty years.'

Now the only people left were Jennie, Peter and, of

course, Kerry, whom Charlie dubbed 'a lovely girl'. It was beginning to look increasingly likely that she might actually win – and the next day it was announced that exactly that had happened, with Peter third, Jennie second and Kerry coming out on top.

Never one to do things by halves, Kerry's reaction was suitably over the top. 'This is brilliant!' she cried as Tara Palmer-Tomkinson, who had been a contestant in the first series and was now a commentator on the show, put a small plastic crown on her head. 'My crown doesn't fit and my legs have gone numb!'

There was more pandemonium when Bryan appeared on the scene. 'Are you proud of me?' asked Kerry?

'My knees have gone, I'm that proud of you,' Bryan replied, and with that the happy couple were escorted to their hotel, before the round of interviews Kerry would be undertaking later in the day.

It was a big moment in Kerry's life, and one of which she was justifiably proud. For a start, those weeks in the jungle really were an ordeal; living conditions were rough, the competitors were frequently left hungry and the Bushtucker Trials were pretty horrible for everyone. But more than that, Kerry had shown herself to be a person in her own right. In the jungle, she emerged from both the shadow of Atomic Kitten and of her husband, love him as she might, to be established as a strong personality in her own right. Some people compared her to Barbara Windsor, another chirpy blonde who had never succumbed to the hard knocks of life; others, newly aware of her background, were simply impressed that she had come through it all.

And now she was Queen of the Jungle, and this had more ramifications than just an empty title – the winner was almost guaranteed their pick of work in the near future at least, with earnings to match. And now that it was all over, Kerry could go home, relax with her husband and see her children. The queen could at long last rest under her crown.

12

QUEEN KERRY I

The nation was gripped. It had been the most successful version ever of *I'm a Celebrity ... Get Me Out of Here!* On the night Kerry won, the show pulled in 15.7 million viewers, 62.2 per cent of the television audience, the biggest ever viewing number for a reality TV show. Kerry herself had offers of work flooding in, as Jan Croxson, of Princess Talent, which represents Kerry, revealed.

'She's had an amazing experience. She wanted to test herself and she's done better than she ever imagined. Lots and lots of people have been telephoning. We have very exciting things to talk to Kerry about but I don't want to say any more until then. We haven't had a chance to see which of these exciting things Kerry will want to do. The first thing Kerry will want to do is to see her kids in Ireland. She'll be really missing them. I'd like Kerry to continue with presenting because she's very good at it. Kerry's a really good comedian and I'd like to see her do more acting.'

Very grubby after two weeks in the jungle, Kerry was allowed back to the hotel for a couple of hours to freshen up, with the ever-attentive Bryan to hand. 'When I got back to the hotel, he washed my back for me,' she related afterwards. 'He washed my hair. He had a bit of a cry, really, when he saw me. He said, "I still feel like you're not here. I'm still missing you."'

Kerry herself was still feeling stunned. 'I'm in shock, gobsmacked, absolutely flabbergasted,' she said. So were a couple of other people, not least the previous winner, Phil Tufnell, who conceded gracefully that she did deserve to win. 'I've made no secret of the fact that I've been critical of Kerry at times,' he said. 'She made a terrible start in the jungle and I thought she wouldn't last five minutes. Kerry seemed to love a good moan and a whinge. But I reckon she will have been the one to have learned most from the experience. She has grown up out there in the jungle and taught herself that she can manage without her family. She's learned to stand on her own two feet. I'm sure Bryan and the girls will be delighted for her and very proud. Kerry has deserved to win and I'm delighted to hand over my crown.'

Bryan's mother Mairead, along with her husband Brendan, had been looking after the children while Bryan and Kerry were away, and they were equally thrilled. When Kerry rang them after getting out of the jungle, Mairead related how affecting the call was. 'She was so emotional.

She broke down and couldn't talk to us,' she said. 'We were her first call when she came out.

'The first thing she said to me when I answered the phone was, "Hi, I cannot believe I missed you all so much." She was absolutely heartbroken on the phone. When I put Molly on, that just finished her altogether. Molly came on and said, "Mummy, Queen of the Jungle…" I'm absolutely knackered now because we had a late night. We are all so happy for her. Any time anybody asked Molly where Mummy was, she'd reply, "In the jungle with the spiders."'

As to why Kerry was the winner, Mairead believed it was because viewers saw the real her. 'What we saw on screen was Kerry,' she said. 'She was natural… apart from all the swearing! When she had a few drinks the other night, I just kept hoping she'd go to bed before she made a show of us! Kerry's more like a daughter to me now than a daughter-in-law. I'm so proud of her.'

So were the Variety Club of Ireland and Temple Street Children's Hospital in Dublin, where Molly had been treated the previous year with suspected meningitis. The two were the beneficiaries of the money Kerry had raised, because she wanted to help disadvantaged children in any way she could. 'If I can give other kids the chance my two have, I'm going to try, and if I fail, I fail,' she told Mairead. 'If I win, I win.'

Helen Cosgrove, who was the fund-raising director for the hospital, said, 'However much she raises will be fantastic. We gave Kerry a wish list before she went. There's everything on there from 10,000 euros up to a million. Everybody in the hospital watched it from day one. We were biting our nails.'

Indeed, Kerry was determined to put her own experiences as a child to good use, and appeared in a BBC1 documentary about children in Care to say she knew just how much it was possible to suffer. 'I've wanted to jump out of windows,' she said. 'I've wanted to die. I've been in places and seen things most people couldn't imagine.' But she had a big message of hope for those children. 'Tomorrow is another day,' she said. 'You don't know what is going to be around the next corner. Want to kill yourself? Don't! The next day may be the most tremendous day you've ever had.'

As for Kerry herself, she was beginning to calm down. 'I'm so happy now,' she said. 'It makes you appreciate everything… like food. I've lost a stone. I know I love Bryan and the kids but being away from them makes you realise how deep it is.' She wasn't even angry when Bryan revealed that he had lost his wedding ring while out surfing, joking only that he had better have travel insurance.

Indeed, Bryan and Kerry were behaving like besotted teenagers, with Bryan telling the world how much he had missed Kerry while she was away. Kerry herself was euphoric to be back with her husband. 'We are trying for another baby now,' she said. 'Who knows just when our wish will come true? But it would be beyond all our dreams, above anything, if it happened now. I was so down [in the jungle] and couldn't see any way up unless I got out. Then I started picturing my girls and Bryan and that brought strength. The love I felt from them just pulled me up and I started to believe I could survive. It was hell out there in the jungle, and during the first couple of days I seriously thought I was about to suffer another nervous breakdown. I have learnt to be a survivor... I have had to be a survivor and that's what helped me win.'

There were, however, some benefits. 'I've gone down two dress sizes and dropped from nine-and-a-half stone to eight-and-a-half stone,' said Kerry. 'I can't believe it. Now I'm going to work to keep it off. Those first two days were awful. I really felt I was going to have a second nervous breakdown. I just thought to myself, 'What am I doing here?' I'd never do it again. I only ever watched it when Phil Tufnell, Linda Barker and Anthony Worrall Thompson were getting drunk and I just thought, "Wow... I'll go on the town with Ant and Dec for two weeks.' I had no idea it would be as tough as it was.

'My worst thing was missing Bryan and the kids. We got there on Tuesday and I just couldn't handle it. I wasn't as bad as what I thought I was going to be on Lilly's first birthday because I took a picture of her in for inspiration. I thought, "All right. Happy birthday, babe. Don't start crying again. Don't start whinging again. You know she's fine. You know she's happy and healthy, now just get on with it." What made it all worthwhile, though, was when my two-year-old daughter Molly came on the phone and said, "Mummy, you're Queen of the Jungle. You've done brilliant."'

Others thought so, too. Kerry's mother Sue was absolutely delighted that her daughter had come through and was cheering her to the rafters. 'I feel ecstatic, amazed and brilliant!' she said. 'I knew she could do it because she's a determined little person – she always has been. She called me after she won, but she didn't say a lot. I just got a "Hiya, Mum," and then she just seemed to be in shock and overcome with it all. She won because she is true to herself. What you see is what you get with Kerry.' And Sue, of course, more than anyone else, understood her daughter's experiences. 'It was only fair she won because she has overcome so much just to even be there,' she said.

And Kerry's foster parents, the Woodalls, were equally pleased. 'She rang me about an hour after she won and simply said, "What do you think?"' said Margaret Woodall. 'I told her I was crying my eyes out, but she was over the moon. It was lovely and she's coming to see us when she gets back.'

Her husband Fred was also thrilled. 'All those years ago when I laughed when she said she would be a star – I couldn't have been more wrong,' he said.

If truth be told, Kerry was still in shock. The contestants were rewarded for their hardship when they came out of the jungle by staying in the five-star Versace Hotel in Surfer's Paradise, a contrast in locations most found quite bizarre. 'I haven't had time to sit down and think about it yet,' said a dazed Kerry. 'It's just dead surreal. I'm absolutely exhausted at the minute. This morning, I just can't remember because it was such a shock. When I was sitting there, I just thought, "It's Jennie." I was sitting knowing I'd cocked up that last challenge and I feel like I cheated everybody really, because

Pete and Jennie really went for it. But at the end of the day, I have nothing to prove to anybody. I said to Jenny, "You're a queen in my eyes." I just felt I'd cheated everybody.'

She was also beginning to relate how she got on with her fellow contestants, revealing that she had become especially close to John (who had subsequently had words with Bryan.) 'He called me his little bunny,' she said. 'He really is one of the most intelligent and interesting men I've ever met. I really hope that we will remain friends. [He was] my favourite. I can't believe he fell out with most people. I want to keep in touch with him.'

Asked for her opinions about some of the others, Kerry didn't have a bad word for anyone. Of Neil she said, 'I cried when he left. I really got on with him. Such a sincere and very kind man.' Mike was 'my Mr Jukebox. A happy member of the family who knew so much about music.' Peter 'was like a younger brother. Very emotional… and the clumsiest person I ever met.' Alex, meanwhile, 'was my older sister. Sweet and caring… lovely. She told me of her personal life.'

Continuing the family theme, Jennie was 'my jungle mum. She never stopped sneaking out to put on make-up but was lovely to me.' Lecherous uncle – although Kerry didn't call him that – was Lord Brocket. 'He was constantly undoing my bra, but in such a cheeky way, I couldn't stay cross for long,' she said. And Diane 'was the most softly-spoken person I've ever met. She is a very open person.'

Of course, the experience had been rewarding for

Kerry – and the others – in another way, too – financially. Kerry had already sold her story to a newspaper for an estimated £200,000, and she was believed to be able to earn at least ten times that in the wake of her win. The others were doing well, too. Lord Brocket had got £1 million from the sale of his autobiography; Peter was hoping to relaunch his singing career; and Jennie had been approached by a variety of cosmetic companies, keen to know if it was their products she had been applying. 'The telephone hasn't stopped ringing,' said her agent Sue Ayton, after Jennie had come out. 'Cosmetics companies have been very interested – they want to know whether it was their product she was using in the jungle and whether it stayed on.'

Kerry herself was uncertain about what she wanted to do next. She really was taken aback by the news that her old friends had gone their separate ways. 'I really feel sad that Atomic Kitten have split, I feel really gutted,' she said. 'I sometimes do wonder what it would have been like had I stayed in the band instead of quitting. I have no idea what I'm going to do career-wise, now. I would go back to singing if I was offered a good solo deal, and there's presenting on the cards. But being in the jungle just makes you appreciate so much more what you have. The experience has really changed me and my outlook. I just want to spend time with the people I love, enjoying every bit of my life.'

Unsurprisingly, Kerry's children were at the forefront of her mind. She had not yet been able to see them, but she just couldn't stop talking about them and what the future held. 'Now I just want to be a good mum and be there for my children,' she said. 'I just want them to grow up to be healthy and happy. I would encourage them to do whatever they wanted to do with their lives. Molly already sings her head off. I have no doubt she will end up on stage. If either of them want to be in a pop band or act, I would just say, "Go for it." I would never want either of them to feel I had held them back. Of course, you do need to learn, but personally I haven't felt a negative impact to fame. But Molly is two-and-a-half and Lilly Sue has just turned one, so there's still a long, long way to go. I love them to bits. I could just eat them.'

Even so, even now, Kerry still sometimes found her background difficult to deal with. 'I do still have to cope with negative feelings… I do still feel unloved sometimes,' she said. 'But I don't express it to anyone, not even Bryan. I just keep it inside. That's what I learnt to do when I was younger. But then I get angry with myself. Why should I feel like that? What I do is I look at my kids and then I feel happy again. The only thing that matters now is what they're feeling. My feelings don't come into consideration any more.'

Now that Kerry had won *I'm a Celebrity…*, everyone was taking an even greater interest in her background than before and, in particular, her relationship with her mother. Kerry was determined, once and for all, to set the record straight. 'When I was younger, she was suffering from manic depression,' Kerry said. 'She is better now. The real turning point for her has been becoming a grandma. She's great now and is getting a chance to make up for what she lost out on with me. It has finally given her happiness.

'I have always had a relationship with my mum. She is a fantastic woman. I can't say anything bad about her. She's had her problems, but she's my mum at the end of the day – she's the only one I've got. I'm having a party in Warrington when I get back. I'll go up there on Friday night and then on Saturday we'll have a big do with the mayor and everything as a welcome home party.'

Such was the euphoria surrounding Kerry's win that Bryan, no less, started to think about an excursion into the jungle himself the following year. A producer of the show had remarked, almost in jest, that Bryan should consider appearing; he actually appeared rather thrilled with the idea. 'I spoke to them about it and all it really depends on is my commitments to the band,' he said. 'Watching Kerry for the first few days was so incredibly hard but, after seeing her triumph, I would just like to give it a go myself. It's a once-in-a-lifetime opportunity. They told me that a new series is already in its planning stages, so I'm just hoping the dates work out.'

Kerry, meanwhile, was the subject of increasing speculation as to what she would do next. She signed a £500,000 deal to promote the Italian pasta company Sacla. 'When I mentioned Sacla, she said she uses it all the time,' said Kerry's indefatigable PR Max Clifford. 'I know she likes Sacla because she has used it when I have had dinner with her. She is natural and saucy and loves Italy.' Commercial as the motives were, that statement did actually sum Kerry up.

There was also some speculation about Kerry either resuming her recording career or, better still – in commercial terms at least – singing a duet with Bryan. 'There are a number of record companies after Kerry to start a solo career,' said one source close to the couple. 'But the really big money offers have been for Kerry and Bryan to do a one-off duet. There's talk of Jordan and Peter Andre doing a song together but Bryan and Kerry are the real romance story of *I'm a Celebrity… Get Me Out of Here!*

'The record companies have been getting songwriters to pen jungle-themed tunes. One that has come up is a love song called 'Your Heart Is a Jungle'. Bryan and Kerry could make a fortune out of this if they wanted to, but they are already very rich so they don't have to do anything they don't want to.' In the event, the record never came off, not least because Bryan was on the verge of making some pretty big career changes of his own.

It was when Kerry returned to Britain that she really appreciated just how much the British public loved her. She went home to Warrington to celebrate her victory, where she was met at the Town Hall by 500 fans who had turned out to congratulate her, all chanting her name. 'This is so overwhelming and I want to thank all of you,' said a clearly overwhelmed Kerry. 'I'm absolutely amazed… I think I'm going to cry again. We had so much fun. It was brilliant, absolutely brilliant, although I would never do it again. It feels fantastic to be Queen of the Jungle. I'm absolutely flabbergasted.' She went on to sign autographs, before going into the building for a civic reception with the Mayor of Warrington, Councillor Pauline Nelson, and members of her family and friends, having finally been reunited with her daughters.

Offers continued to come in. The next was the suggestion that Kerry and Bryan should take part in *Celebrity Wife Swap* opposite Kerry's jungle friend Neil Ruddock and his wife Sarah. 'That would be great,' said an enthusiastic Kerry. 'Me and Razor [Neil's nickname] could go on the piss for two weeks together. I love *Wife Swap* and, like the rest of the nation, I always watched the last series. It was fantastic television. I would love to see how it all turned out and I think me and Neil would have a great laugh doing the programme. Bryan is up for it, too, and it was actually his idea in the first place. When I was still in the jungle, Razor and Bryan were having a boozy session in the hotel. They decided it would be great to do a wife swap because Neil was so good at looking after me when we were in the jungle.'

As for Bryan entering the jungle himself, however, Kerry put the rumours to bed. 'No, he's not… he couldn't hack it. He wouldn't last long with so little food and with all the bugs everywhere. There is no way he is going to go into the jungle – and I would miss him too much again anyway.'

As *I'm a Celebrity…* fever continued, the next stop was

London, where Kerry had been invited to present an award at the Brits. It was, unfortunately, not an unqualified success. Kerry herself was as popular as ever, but a comment she made did not go down well in the press – 'You look so clean and smell lovely,' she said, 'and I've just farted.' Quite a few people – including, allegedly, Bryan – were not amused and there were rumours the two of them had a row afterwards and that Bryan was seen chatting someone up. It was the very first sign of the public discord that was to come.

Initially, however, the two were keen to gloss over what had happened, denying point-blank that there had been any chatting up or any rows. 'I went to the Brits. I didn't really get to enjoy them as I was there to present an award,' said Kerry. 'We'd also invited Charlie Brocket and so we were looking after him,' added Bryan. 'We brought him along with us to the BMG party afterwards.'

'Apparently, someone at the party rang the press up,' Kerry continued. 'The room was crowded and I was loving everyone coming up to me and congratulating me, but I was so knackered. It'd been non-stop since I got off the plane from Australia. I just got to the point where I couldn't say one more "Oh, thank you very much". So I just wanted to go home to bed. I didn't actually tell Bryan I was going home.' The couple went on to explain that Bryan then rang Kerry, who, in turn, told him to stay on and enjoy himself. They were adamant; there had been no row.

But there was just a little bit of tension evident between

them when they discussed Kerry's Brit appearance. 'I actually really, really regret saying that I farted when I got up on stage,' said Kerry.

'Because it wasn't necessary?' asked Bryan.

'I just really regret it,' said Kerry.

'Were you thinking about saying it before you went on? I told you about doing that before,' said Bryan.

'I know, but I still did it,' said a penitent Kerry. 'If I think of things to be funny, they're not funny, whereas I'm normally a really spontaneous person.'

'If you have ever watched Kerry on a long television show, like *Parkinson*,' said Bryan, softening slightly, 'that's where she's best as she's off the cuff and she's herself.' No more was said at the time, but there had been a distinct chill in the air.

The pair were still besotted enough for Bryan to be writing songs for Kerry, however; he had just penned a number called 'If My World Stopped Turning', in which he spoke, yet again, of his love for her. But there was another change, one that the couple had perhaps not fully come to terms with, although people were beginning to ask about it. In simple terms, whenever Kerry spoke about wanting to step out from the shadow of Atomic Kitten and, indeed, of Bryan, the truth was, she had finally succeeded.

Ever since she'd won *I'm a Celebrity…*, the papers had been full of news and features about Kerry – and not about Bryan. For once, he was playing the supporting role in the marriage, rather than the other way round. It had all been so sudden that neither seemed to be aware that the balance of power had shifted, but the fact was that Kerry was now a celebrity in her own right – and perhaps there was just a small part of Bryan that didn't like it.

Whatever Bryan's feelings about Kerry's growing fame, he was soon back in the headlines himself. For years now, Bryan had been complaining about the downside of being in Westlife – the constant touring and travelling, the ceaseless schedule and life on the road – and it had finally taken its toll. In the beginning of March 2004, just a month after Kerry came out of the jungle, Bryan announced that he was leaving the band in order to spend more time with Kerry and the children. First, rumours began to circulate on the Internet and then Bryan confirmed that they were true at a packed press conference, at which he was accompanied by Kerry.

'It's a huge commitment and, to be honest, for the last year, especially since Lilly was born, I haven't been able to commit 100 per cent to Westlife and I haven't been able to commit 100 per cent to my family,' he said. 'It wasn't fair on either and I just felt it was the right time for me to leave and concentrate on my family. The guys want me to be happy. My family are very important to me and they understand that. There's no point in being in the band and not having 100 per cent commitment, so they respect my decision.'

Indeed, everyone was extremely keen to emphasise that the break was completely amicable. The four remaining members of Westlife released a statement in return, which was read out by Kian: 'We have enjoyed some unbelievable times throughout the years and will always hold them and you very close to our hearts,' he said. 'We have shared laughter, tears, success, weddings and babies, but most of all we've shared our dreams.'

Nicky stepped forward to ask for the fans' continuing support – the group was not breaking up, after all, but merely continuing as a four-piece without Bryan. 'At this moment we just hope the fans stay with us… we need them now more than ever,' he said.

Bryan's departure from the group almost immediately heralded huge changes in the rest of his life. For a start, he switched back to spelling his name 'Brian', as it had been before he joined the band. Weight fell off. His hair changed from blond to brown, grew long and a beard appeared. He was making every conceivable attempt to show that a new chapter had begun in his life.

'It was the Atkins diet,' Brian explained, when talking about his dramatic new look. 'I started it when I was in Westlife and I just carried on when I left and lost three stone. I was fifteen stone before and I'd be trying to play football but I was just unfit.' As for everything else, Brian was nonchalant; he had been going to meet Anthony Costa from Blue in a pub and instead ended up at a film première after-show party, looking somewhat scruffier than was his wont. The subsequent pictures made headlines.

'Anthony was standing there in a suit and I'm proper scraggy in this T-shirt I've had since I was fifteen,' he said. 'It wasn't a conscious change at all. In Westlife, I had a stylist who did my hair every day and, when I left, I obviously no longer had that privilege. And I haven't shaved because I shaved every day of my life in Westlife… you have to.'

At first, Brian spoke a lot about his desire to stay at home with his wife and children, but almost immediately it became clear that he was as determined to have a solo career as successful as his stint with Westlife. Kerry, meanwhile, was no slouch either. On the back of the success of *I'm a Celebrity…*, she was more in demand than ever and jetting all over the world to fulfil her contractual obligations. Kerry – who had been as surprised as anyone by Brian's decision to quit – was asked if it was easier for the family now that he'd left the band; the answer was telling.

'It's been a lot harder, to be honest with you,' she said. 'It's funny, but I saw a lot more of him when he was in Westlife. We've both been working hard. It's sad really; it'd be nice to see more of each other. We seem to get on better on the phone.'

Behind the scenes, pressures were beginning to show and Kerry also admitted to the odd problem in the relationship. 'There are strains in our marriage. We're human beings,' she said. 'No matter how much we love each other, we have to work at it. We have little tiffs all the time about stupid little things like leaving glasses on the worktop. Bryan's worst habit is leaving towels on the floor.' She also grumbled that Brian was less romantic than he used to be – but by that stage, the couple had been married for over two years and had been together for years before that. Every relationship loses its initial white heat of intensity, so there appeared to be nothing more wrong than that.

And the two still seemed very much together. They were continuing to talk about having more children, and Brian was writing songs for Kerry. He was also being spoken of as a future Robbie Williams, which cannot have displeased him at all. And Kerry was not only doing presenting work, she had started going to auditions and was hoping to branch out into acting in the near future. From the outside, at least, nothing appeared to be wrong. But changes were afoot – and over the coming months, Kerry was going to have to cope with the heartbreak of a marriage that was showing all the signs of disintegration.

13

TROUBLE BREWING

Life for Brian really had changed. Apart from leaving Westlife, he had given up drinking, was talking about giving up smoking and had lost a staggering amount of weight. But an undercurrent of tension was still apparent. In one interview, Kerry related that they had had words: 'We had a bit of a row this morning,' she said. 'It was about the usual, petty married stuff. We're both godparents at a christening, so I told him to put the date in his diary and he said, "I can't in case something pops up," and I said, "Well, just tell your managers that you've got to have that day off." It's not hard, is it?'

Brian released his first solo single, 'Real To Me', which went to Number One, but that seemed to do little to dispel the sense that there were real problems emerging. In another interview, Kerry was less sanguine about the changes in her husband's life, and didn't seem entirely content with her own. 'I just work my ass off,' she grumbled. 'I run around after two kids and a husband and work hard. I still worry about Brian on the Atkins diet because he's loving all the compliments he's getting, but I think it's really unhealthy.'

Even so, no one was prepared for what happened next. The split, when it came, seemed to happen almost overnight. One minute Kerry and Brian were the golden couple of pop: the next, they were separating.

It looked like there had been long term consequences from the lap-dancing incident. To many, Kerry and Brian appeared to have put it behind them, but the reality was that Kerry had still not been able to get over the betrayal of trust. 'To the outside world, it looked like Brian and Kerry had kissed and made up over that whole stag-night encounter,' said a friend. 'But it came back to haunt him over and over again. They would have huge screaming matches about it and it would always come back to the same thing – trust.

'Kerry is big on trust. She's had a lot of upset in her life and she needs to feel people around her are 100 per cent loyal. Brian would get really upset about it. He'd say that he loved her, she knew that the stag-night incident didn't mean anything.' But what would be the real repercussions?

Nor did it help that the couple were barely seeing one another. Brian was going all out to make his solo career a success, while Kerry was doing the same with her acting.

'I'd left Westlife to spend more time with my wife Kerry and our two kids, but ironically they happened to be away on the day that "Real To Me" hit the top,' said Brian. 'I was all alone. And, in fact, I've seen less of Kerry since I quit the band, because for three months she's been in County Galway making a film called *Showbands*.'

Kerry, however, was absolutely and utterly devastated, leaving Ireland with the two girls to take refuge with her mother Sue in Warrington. Indeed, her grief was palpable. 'Brian left me,' she said, in her first words on the subject. 'He's not listening to anything I have to say. As far as he is concerned, our marriage is over. Brian has told me that there is no one else and that is the situation as far as I know.'

Everyone rallied round. Sue said that Kerry and Brian had been speaking on the phone, adding, 'Kerry is trying to sort things out with Brian. She hasn't seen him and is staying with me for the time being. I've been supporting her.'

Kerry's foster mother Margaret Woodall was hopeful that matters could be repaired. 'They've had a series of rows but I'm sure their split is just a temporary one,' she said. 'Kerry is a very strong girl, but her family is the most important thing in her life. And anyone who sees them together as a family knows that Brian is devoted to her and the girls. She came back to Warrington because she needs the support of her friends and family.'

But, alas, Brian had very different ideas. 'It's not likely we'll get back together. We'll divorce,' he said. 'But we haven't talked details because, at the moment, for the sake of the kids, we just want to get our lives straight. We had issues, things came to a head, and we split. I do talk to Kerry on the phone, but not for long and we only talk about the girls. I always call to say goodnight to them and I find it very hard because I miss them. Afterwards, I'm in tears. I love them so much, and it hurts.'

Meanwhile, it seemed Kerry was absolutely distraught. 'Kerry is devastated,' said Sue, who was clearly very worried about her daughter. 'She was hysterical and has been sobbing her heart out. Brian hasn't given her a reason, so she's saying, "Maybe he doesn't fancy me, maybe it's because I'm fat, is it because of how my body's changed?" But she's had two kids, for goodness sake. She is wondering whether, if she loses weight, it will bring him back. Kerry's not eating because she is so stressed and she's been having panic attacks. It's killing her. It all started three weeks ago. Brian phoned Kerry and said he didn't love her. Since then, Kerry keeps saying, "Why is Brian doing this? What have I done?" In another phone call, she shouted at Brian, "I've given you five years and you end it on the phone. Is that all I'm worth?"' In a later interview, Brian would hotly deny that he had ended the relationship with a phone call.

One person who was prepared to talk on Kerry's behalf was her childhood friend Michelle Hunter, who also revealed quite how unexpected Brian's behaviour had been. Kerry had been constantly in tears, she said, unable to understand why this had happened, and she simply wanted to repair the damage that had been done. 'Kerry is an absolute wreck,' she said. 'All she keeps asking is "Why?" She just wants to know what she's done that's so wrong that Brian doesn't want to be with her any more. There is just no reason for the break-up. There's certainly no one else involved with Kerry and she won't even discuss the possibility of Brian ditching her for somebody else. Kerry doesn't want to divorce Brian. She adores him and wants him back, no matter how much this is hurting her now.'

Sue continued to look after her daughter, and explained what she thought had gone wrong. Kerry had, after all, given up Atomic Kitten just before the group hit the big time and it had been earlier in the year when she finally came into her own. '*I'm A Celebrity…* gave Kerry a second chance,' she said. 'But I think her success pissed Brian off. Suddenly, he was in the shade and was being invited to things as Kerry's guest. Brian has become self-obsessed. The words of his song ['Real To Me'] are laughable. It is like he is going through a mid-life crisis and wants his freedom back. He is thinking to himself, "Is the grass greener on the other side?" Maybe he wants to go and sow his wild oats, but, if he did, Kerry wouldn't take him back. I wouldn't let her.'

Brian himself claimed that Kerry's growing fame had nothing to do with his decision. 'The reason Kerry and I split is because of personal reasons, not because of our workload,' he said. 'Kerry winning *I'm A Celeb…* and rising to fame again had nothing to do with it. I was so proud and happy for her. That was never a problem.

'One of the main reasons I wanted to leave Westlife and

go home was because I was missing my kids. Being away from them and missing them growing up was killing me. And also, not having the perfect marriage either wasn't helping. So, in my head, I was thinking that, maybe if I have more time at home, we can fix it and make it better. But, to be honest, I think when I left Westlife for the first month or two we did spend all our time together and it just didn't get better.

'I still love Kerry to bits, and I want her to be happy. I spoke to her last night and she's in great form. But I wasn't happy and then how can I make my family happy? It just got to the stage where when I came home there was no happy atmosphere and when that's gone... We're only 24, it's not like we're married for 20 years. You've just got to be happy.'

The fact, of course, was that Kerry was not.

Brian had also been linked with someone else: ex-Neighbours star Delta Goodrem, with whom he had done some work. He firmly denied that anything was going on. 'That is ridiculous,' he said. 'She's a friend and we've done a duet. Yes, I've spoken to her a few times since the split – but as a friend. There's no way that she's a shoulder to cry on or anything like that. There have been all sorts of stupid rumours. I was supposed to have got off with Cheryl Tweedy from Girls Aloud earlier in the year. Rubbish!'

Max Clifford, Kerry's publicist, confirmed that she had sought specialist help. 'She is a very emotional girl anyway and the split with Brian has been very hard for her to handle,' he said. 'She is just very down and the doctor at

Harley Street said the best thing for her to do was get down there for a few days. Brian has got the children. That is what has been going on for two months. He has them and then she has them.'

Finally, and seemingly inevitably, the last chapter of Kerry and Brian's relationship as a married couple was played out when it emerged that Brian and Delta were indeed a couple. Both had been denying it for months, and both steadily maintained that they only got together on December 2004, when they duetted at a Royal Variety Show, but, whatever the truth, they were pictured on holiday in Cape Town over the New Year, which confirmed that they were now undoubtedly together.

Brian himself was thought to have told Kerry his news on Christmas Eve, and, once out, he was open about it. 'It was the hardest conversation of my life, telling Kerry I was in love with someone else,' he said. 'This was the final nail. I don't love her any more and we're not right for each other. Delta and I are an item.'

But it was not how Kerry had expected to be celebrating the New Year. Divorce is always traumatic and, in this case, given that the split was totally unexpected, Kerry had had shock to deal with as well as the pain of her marriage breaking up. But time and again she has proved her resilience and, as the months wore on, she yet again proved herself able to cope. 'I want a new man for Christmas,' she announced on ITV1's *This Morning*. 'New chapter, new hair – and maybe a new man for Christmas, you never know.'

Certainly, the change in her appearance was striking. Those famous curves were still present, but in a radically thinner version, while her hair was now a glossy brunette. She had also started undergoing laser surgery to remove the tattoo of Brian's name from her back. And Kerry was now back living in Warrington, finding comfort from familiar surroundings, and resolutely determined to put the recent past behind her.

Now that she was single, there was certainly no shortage of admirers. Over the Christmas period, Kerry agreed to take a short break in Spain with the reality-television star Fran Cosgrave, who was a Westlife bodyguard – and who, to complicate matters still further, had had a child with another Atomic Kitten, Natasha Hamilton. Fran himself, however, was adamant that he was only there to help. He had supported Kerry as she was battling with depression and now clearly felt that she needed a break. 'I'll do anything for Kerry – she introduced me to Natasha, the love of my life,' he said. 'I suggested we go on holiday and Kerry smiled and said she would love to. She deserves a break and sometimes you need a strong shoulder to lean on.' In the event, nothing came of the holiday.

Her career was still going well: she was on excellent form as Marilyn Monroe on *Celebrity Stars In Their Eyes*, and she had transformed herself into a 1960s singer, complete with beehive, for the Irish drama *Showbands*, in which she played Denise, a cleaning lady in a pub, who teams up with a showband manager to work her way up to the musical stage.

And, despite everything that had happened over the past few months, Kerry retained the down-to-earth qualities that had so endeared her to the public. In January, she took part in a programme called *My Fair Kerry*, in which she was given two weeks' etiquette training in order to try to pass herself off as a member of the upper classes. 'This is a new year and a new start for me,' she said. 'I admit my table manners and Ps and Qs aren't up to scratch and that I burp in public.'

As an indication of how well known Kerry had become, the programme was made in Austria, because she would have been too easily recognised in the UK.

Quite how much the public supported Kerry, and not Brian, in what had turned into a publicity war, became clear in February. Brian and Delta performed their song 'Almost Here' at the Meteor Awards in Dublin, but the occasion did not go as planned: the pair were booed by the audience. The message was clear: they felt Brian had behaved very badly towards Kerry and they were not going to accept another woman in her place without making their feelings known.

Kerry's other work continued. She had been made an ambassador for The Prince's Trust, the organisation set up by Prince Charles to help the underprivileged, and appeared very much to have her life back on track. She also had a new boyfriend – or rather, an old one – Dave Cunningham, a local decorator Kerry had been at school with, and had gone out with briefly in the past.

Her friends were a great help, especially Lisa and Joanne,

who did a great deal for her while she was being treated for depression. 'I can't express how much support I've had from them,' said a grateful Kerry in an interview. 'They have been amazing. When I was in the Priory, Lisa and Joanne moved all my furniture into my new house and sorted all my clothes out for me. That's the kind of friends they are. When I got back home, everything was organised for me. They drove me and the kids everywhere. While I was away filming, Lisa and her boyfriend looked after the girls and Joanne took them for days out.'

Further good news followed when Kerry won the Celebrity Mum of the Year award – for the second time. 'For the first time in my life I'm truly gobsmacked,' said a delighted Kerry. 'I'm so chuffed to receive this award. Molly and Lilly will be so proud of their mummy. It's [the separation] a big difference and it can be a little hard, but they do see their daddy. The good thing about my job is that I can plan it around my girls.'

There was a breakthrough of sorts in the spring when Kerry and Brian actually met each other, both accompanied by their new partners. The venue was the Radisson Hotel in Galway for a flight launch by Club 328/EuroManx to Malaga, and both Kerry and Brian were on the VIP guest list. Kerry was accompanied by Dave and Brian by Delta – and by his former bandmate Nicky Byrne as well, drafted in to produce some much needed moral support. It was a momentous occasion for both of them.

'This is a massive move for the two of them after what's

been an incredibly tough six months,' said an insider. 'Bri and Kerry are emotional people and after the split they both said things they regret. They're happily in love with new people now and want to try and be friends, at the very least because that will make things easier for their children, Molly and Lilly-Sue. Kerry is a lot happier with the situation now because things are going really well with Dave. He's supposed to be moving into her Warrington home, so no doubt she wanted to show the world she's moved on.'

It had been a tough time for Kerry and it was about to get tougher still. She had hardly even begun to recover from the devastation of her divorce than she was the subject of newspaper allegations brought by her old friend Joanne. It was unclear exactly what had happened between them, although it was obviously an almighty falling out, but the upshot was that Joanne claimed that Kerry was a drug user, with an addiction to cocaine.

'Kerry is killing herself with cocaine,' she claimed to *News of the World*. 'It's like she doesn't care about anything when she's on it. She binges on cocaine for days on end without sleep. It's almost as if she wants to self-destruct. One night I found her in such a state she was screaming about the curtains talking to her. She needs help.'

But, this time round, Kerry came out fighting. Incensed by such allegations and, perhaps, stronger within herself than she had been after Brian walked out, she refuted the allegations with an energy fuelled by rage. 'Do I look like a class-A-drug user?' she demanded 'I don't think so. I'm hyper enough – I don't need to take drugs. Oxygen is enough. It just goes to show you don't know who your real friends are sometimes. But I'm not going to let it affect me or my two kids. I've done nothing wrong. I'm going to carry on holding my head up high.'

In many ways, she was looking better than ever. The stress of the last few months meant that the weight just dropped off, with Kerry now back down to a petite size eight. 'I always say to Brian, "I'm grateful for one thing. I've got my figure back,"' she said. 'I know it sounds stupid and vain, but after having two kids I put on so much weight, then lost it, and there was so much saggy skin. When the man you love says he doesn't love you, your ego does get a bit knocked. After I came out of the Priory, I thought, "All right, I've got a new house, got a new car, got a new man. Go for new hair, new body, new life, new start. The past is gone. Move on." I got rid of my married name, too, although it kills me that I'm never going to have the same name as my kids.'

Brian also spoke publicly about the fallout from his broken marriage. 'I do think I've copped an enormous amount of shit in the past few months,' he said, in a slightly belated damage-limitation exercise. 'There was no way that I expected what's happened, that it would all be so black and white; that there'd be a good guy and a bad guy and I'd be the bad guy. What did I do to be painted as the villain? I don't know. Probably being born.'

Possibly the most harmful allegation that had been made

about Brian was that he had split up with Kerry over the telephone, which bespoke a real heartlessness, and naturally he was very keen to quash that rumour completely. 'They said I rang her up one day and said, "It's over," but that would just be inhumane,' he said. 'How anyone can believe something like that is incredible. I'm not a monster, it's ridiculous. How could anyone believe that I could break up a four-year relationship and a marriage over the phone? It's just so obvious it's not true.'

Kerry was showing every sign of wanting to settle down again herself once the parting from Brian was finally formalised. 'I would actually marry Dave tomorrow if he asked me,' she said. 'But I have to get divorced first of all. We are both definite about getting married. Dave is fantastic with the kids and he gets on well with my ex. We would definitely want a child together. I've said I want to do stuff right this time and get married before I have any more babies. But we would love to have a little boy. Dave is such a good man and we are best friends. He's a fantastic guy. We both want the same things in life and that's really important. He understands me and was a great friend during a very tough time and that brought us closer together.'

But the tough time for Kerry was not yet over. The past few months had taken their toll, especially the allegations about cocaine. And it was not so much the allegations themselves as the person who made them that devastated Kerry: after surviving a fractured childhood and forming what she thought had been a secure relationship, not only had she seen her marriage break up unexpectedly, but also she had an erstwhile friend making allegations in the press as well.

She would not have been human if she hadn't been affected by it all, and affected she certainly was: after another stay in the Priory, she finally decided to bite the bullet and go to a place known for its excellent treatment of people with severe problems. And so it was that she ended up in the Meadows clinic in Arizona, which had also treated such troubled stars as Tara Palmer-Tomkinson in the past, while Brian looked after the children. In total, Kerry spent three weeks at the clinic.

After all the travails of the recent past, Kerry needed to take her mind off her problems, and she certainly got that opportunity in September. Jordan became Mrs Peter Andre in a ceremony that ensured maximum coverage, and, although it was not her day, Kerry, a bridesmaid, was in the middle of it all.

It certainly was quite an event. Jordan wore a pink wedding dress, topped off with a tiara, and arrived at the ceremony in a horse-drawn carriage, which looked very much like Cinderella's pumpkin. Her bridesmaids were Kerry and Sarah Harding from Girls Aloud. The ceremony itself was held at Highclere Castle, near Newbury, in Berkshire and, despite being dubbed by some commentators as the 'Chav wedding of the year', it still produced a great deal of good cheer for everyone involved.

But, for some reason, the public bust-ups continued. Kerry was well on her way back to health and happiness, but, like so many stars before her, she discovered that she simply could not steer clear of controversy, try as she might. The latest problem to make itself felt was a row with her former friend Michelle Hunter: Kerry believed that Michelle had been trying to sell stories about her and so, when the two bumped into one another at Dublin Airport in December 2005, a nasty row broke out. And, like so much else, it was soon all over the papers.

It was certainly an ugly scene. Michelle claimed that Kerry hit her with her suitcase, before being restrained by other people in the arrivals lounge. 'Kerry was screaming at the top of her voice, "You're dead, you best be scared because you know I'll do it,"' she said.

But Kerry was adamant that it was not her fault. 'I was minding my own business and then Michelle shouted an abusive comment at me as I got off the plane,' she said. I couldn't contain my rage. That's when I turned around and told her to get out of my way. She's still angry at me because I have cut her out of my life since the summer.'

Michelle's sister Claire also entered the fray but on Kerry's side. 'Kerry has done everything to help my sister over the years,' she said. 'When Michelle was going to be living on the streets because she couldn't pay for her rent Kerry came to her rescue and saved her by giving her money. When Michelle's baby was born Kerry was the one who went out with her and bought her first pram because she couldn't afford it.'

Matters were not helped when Kerry revealed that, like

her mother, she had been diagnosed as a manic depressive. 'The doctors told me it's hereditary,' she said. 'They said it's manic depression and also known as bipolar disorder. When I left rehab in Arizona I was still really tearful. The doctors told me I should be feeling more positive. I was on antidepressants but still crying. It was a relief when they diagnosed bipolar. I thought I was going insane.'

And, of course, all this was taking its toll on Kerry's relationship with Dave. Already stressed out by the rows with Brian, the public tiffs and the depression, Kerry's relationship with her new man had become very volatile: one minute on, the next not. At times the couple seemed in danger of splitting for good, but that Christmas they decided they would make a real effort to keep it together. Unfortunately, it was not to last.

There was yet more controversy on another visit to Ireland when she appeared on Ryan Tubridy's television show and was accused of having had too much to drink beforehand after she appeared a little slurred. Again, this was point blank denied. 'She only had half a glass of wine when she arrived at the show,' said her spokesman. 'She had a mouth abscess and probably found it hard to talk.'

Still in Dublin, Kerry attended an after-show party in Lillie's Bordello after the Meteor Awards, when she was attacked by a fellow reveller. The situation got so out of hand security guards had to rescue her. 'The bitch tried to pull my hair out and start a fight with me,' said a shaken Kerry afterwards. 'She was trying to grab me by my dress.

I don't even know who she is. I can't believe it. I was waiting for my friend to come back from the toilet so I rested my head on my handbag.

'I closed my eyes and the next minute there was this girl trying to pull me up on to my feet. I wasn't even drinking. I was only having a rest until my friend came back. She was really vicious and it hurt me. I told her to get off but she kept pulling at me. We were pushing each other and I was screaming at her to get off. I could not believe what was happening. Thankfully, the bouncers jumped in and really protected me. The girl is obviously absolutely crazy.'

It was a very unfortunate end to the evening. But worse was to come when the scene was repeated just a couple of days later back in Warrington. Kerry was out with friends at a bar called Panama Jacks, when she was set upon by someone else there. 'Kerry was in Panama Jacks with a group of mates when it all kicked off,' said an onlooker. 'Kerry had only walked through the door when some girl started hassling her and insulting her. Kerry wasn't very happy about it and told her to clear off. When she refused there was a huge scuffle and Kerry's hair extensions were pulled out.'

Max Clifford explained what had happened. 'Kerry was having a drink with friends when a girl came up and started abusing her,' he said. 'She was obviously drunk, so Kerry said to her, "Look, love, it's not my fault you're drunk or you're ugly." The girl then went for Kerry and she hit her in self-defence. She was escorted from the premises and Kerry continued to enjoy her night with her friends.'

In fact, this was not quite the end of it: Kerry was arrested and cautioned after the event.

Kerry and Dave finally split shortly after Christmas, but she was not single for long. Just a few weeks later, she was seen at the Chicago Rock Café with Mark Croft, a cab driver nine years her senior who lived just under two miles away from where Kerry was based. And, right from the start, they seemed to be hitting it off extremely well. 'Kerry and Mark were in the VIP area,' said a friend. 'They were with some other mates, but it was obvious they were together. They were laughing and joking and frequently touched hands.'

Events moved extraordinarily fast after that. A mere five weeks later, the couple got engaged and Mark revealed the circumstances: 'We were lying in bed when I said to Kerry, "I could marry you,"' he revealed. 'She said, "We have to get engaged and we need a ring."'

And so they did. Mark duly found the ring, enlisted the help of Kerry's mother to have it fitted with a larger diamond and the two became formally engaged.

14

MRS MARK

In hindsight, it is easy to see that Kerry's real problems began after the split with Brian. With a background like hers, what she needed more than anything was security: what she got was yet another person she trusted letting her down. The haste with which she became engaged to Mark also spoke of her need to have someone to rely on. Meanwhile, after months of denial, the full extent of her self-destructive behaviour was beginning to become apparent.

'I was drinking and doing drugs because that was all I could think of because my life was such a mess,' she confessed. 'Rather than think I had to sort my life out and deal with all my problems, I just fucked myself up even more with cocaine and booze; I was completely out of control. When people found out how I was behaving I didn't really care but it broke my heart that I was being called an unfit mother.'

The engagement to Mark was announced in March 2006, causing a great deal of surprise to friends of Kerry's who worried whether Mark was the right man for her.

A rather poignant insight was offered by Kerry herself, speaking to *Heat* magazine. 'You know I'd give anything for the kids to have their daddy living with me and have the family together,' she said rather sadly. 'I don't speak to Brian. He has his life, I have my life. He sees the kids when he can. I wish him all the love and happiness – he is Molly and Lilly's father.'

And as for being over him – 'I have my days,' she said. 'My family got destroyed – it got split up. When Brian left me, it broke me and I had a nervous breakdown.

'I didn't go out and I started drinking a hell of a lot. I was depressed, and, before I started getting too drunk, I went away to get a little help. I was crying all the time. I couldn't stop. Brian was with me and took me to the Priory. I couldn't sleep because Brian wasn't with me. My whole world had just shattered around me. I was trying to put on a brave face and pretend, "I'm fine, I'm fine, I'm fine."

'I would just go out constantly and have fun. I didn't want the kids to see I was crying all the time. It was like, "I'm getting divorced and everyone knows about me."'

It hardly spelled a promising future with Mark, but Kerry was adamant that she was now far more in love with him than she had ever been with her ex. 'He does everything for me – he's totally ace,' she said. 'I've never felt as loved or as cared for by anyone as much as I do now. He's dead funny and he really makes me laugh, but I hated him the first time I met him. He was a friend of my mum's and I just didn't like him at all. Then, when I started seeing him more, I said to my mum, "I've got a weird crush on him."'

Her mum would later have revelations of her own about Mark. But, even as Kerry was speaking of their burgeoning relationship, an interview with Mark's live-in girlfriend, Louise Oortwyn, with whom he already had a child, surfaced in *News of the World* claiming that he had left her for Kerry. These allegations were hotly denied by Kerry and Mark, who said the couple had split 18 months previously. But again, this did not bode well for the future.

Despite reports of rows and splits, Kerry and Mark pressed ahead and in April held an engagement party. It was all a little bizarre. The party itself took place at a budget hotel, Best Western Hotel, and Kerry revealed to the 200 guests present that she was a bit strapped for cash. 'People think I've got loads of money,' she declared. 'I might have a few pairs of Gina shoes, but I'm skint.' Gesturing to her dress, she continued, 'It was £12.99 from the market, but it will do, won't it.'

No one seemed to know quite what to make of it all.

Kerry was also in a defiant mood about the speed at which the relationship had progressed. 'Everyone is still thinking about me and Brian,' she protested (and with good reason, given the interview she'd given just weeks before). 'But I'd only met Brian about three weeks before he proposed to me. I love Mark and I'm fine. It'll be fine –

well, as soon as I get a divorce. I can't see us lasting 50 years. But I've got a nice ring for now, anyway.' It was hardly the most encouraging comment for a lifetime of wedded bliss.

Nor was Brian appearing to make things easier for his ex to wed. The divorce had still not formally come through and it didn't look as if it was going to for a while yet, either. Kerry told friends, 'This is it, I truly don't know how I lived without Mark before; he does everything for me. I'm just waiting for my divorce to come through in a few months and then we'll definitely do it. I can't wait. Brian is in no rush for the divorce and he's keeping me from marrying Mark. There is paperwork that could have been completed months ago but he won't play ball. I'm desperate to marry Mark.'

Still, however, her friends expressed concern, not least Jordan. 'I don't believe in it [the wedding] if you want to know the truth,' she said. 'Kerry's similar to me, she just wants to be loved, and any time a man shows her affection she's grabbing it. I think she shouldn't keep dashing into new relationships and that she should make certain she's happy with herself first.'

However, that didn't seem very likely. A new row had reportedly broken out with Brian over access to the children, while Kerry was beginning to feel that a clean break from Warrington was needed. It was her hometown, but the various reports of her complicated lifestyle meant that she had to endure taunts on the street. 'I've advised Kerry to move out of Warrington because at the moment she's like a big fish in a small pond,' said her spokesman

Max Clifford. 'It will help her to move on with her life if she leaves Warrington.'

There were even reports that Brian was offering to buy her a new home in Ireland, although, given the history between them, Kerry wasn't very likely to accept that. Meanwhile, Brian, who had been living in New York with Delta, was said to be returning to Ireland himself so that he could be closer to his girls.

The war of words rapidly escalated. Although Brian wasn't prepared to speak out himself (probably wisely), he allowed a friend to do so for him in *The Mirror*. 'This has to stop,' he said. 'Kerry's stories about Brian are making him out to be a bad dad. She claimed Brian never makes any effort to see his kids and sent them home from a visit to New York on a plane – but they were with their godmother on that flight. That's how low Kerry has sunk. The girl needs help. She has actually started believing her own stories.

'I have personally seen how Brian spends weekends in hotels in London and Manchester just to have the girls. Only a few weeks ago he checked into a Manchester hotel for three days so he could get access to the girls. Delta stayed too and they all had a fantastic weekend. Brian decided to bring Molly and Lilly-Sue on a trip to New York to see where he lived a fortnight ago. He took them to *Beauty And The Beast*, a day in Central Park and to the zoo. They had a ball and then their godmother Marilyn flew back home with them.

'When the girls go back to Kerry, they cry and say they are missing their dad, which is natural enough. But Kerry was so jealous the girls had such a good time that she told newspapers he made them travel without someone they were familiar with. But it's not as if it was a stranger. It's a disgusting way to behave because the woman she was talking about was actually her own bridesmaid. What kind of a person would do a thing like that? Kerry makes out in all the papers and magazines that she is so happy with her new life. But I've been with Brian when he gets the messages and phone calls and they are really vicious at times. Brian just ignores them but Kerry is still trying to pester him with nasty messages. She is obviously furious he has made a life for himself with Delta. She says she can't live without her new man Mark, so why is she so hung up on Brian?' Why indeed?

It didn't take long for Brian to speak out himself, however. Kerry was pictured stumbling out of a London nightclub clearly the worse for wear, prompting another blast from her ex. 'She sends letters to my lawyers while the kids are in Warrington and she's in a bar in London with her latest fiancé,' he raged to Heat. 'I am appealing for full custody of the kids as she is an unfit mother who is using our kids as a weapon. Kerry is stopping me from seeing the girls. Every time I organise time to be with them she sends me lawyers' letters making demands that she knows will make it physically impossible to meet.'

Kerry's response was icy. 'The last thing I would want is

for Brian not to see the children,' she said pointedly. 'I lost out myself on not having a father around when I grew up and would naturally hate for my daughters to experience what I went through. Having said that, with them in school Brian should not expect to see them at the drop of a hat wherever and whenever it suits him.'

It seemed Brian was not prepared to give in, and matters soon took an even nastier turn. 'Kerry can let this go all the way to court if she wants but I'm prepared to tell the truth about what kind of a person she is and it would be fireworks,' he said. 'It would shock people and I know for a fact any judge would rule in my favour that the girls should be with me. I've spoken to my legal advisers and they have told me I have a very good chance of getting full custody of the girls and that is what I am aiming to do.'

Kerry responded to this by saying she'd die without her children and publicly called on the two of them to stop the slanging match, which seemed to calm matters temporarily.

Then, in July 2006 Kerry announced that she was expecting her first child with Mark, and they were thrilled. 'Kerry was gobsmacked when she learned she was expecting,' said Max Clifford. 'She was on holiday in Marbella and her tummy was a bit swollen, so she went to the doctor. She phoned me as soon as she got back and was over the moon. She and Mark are delighted with the news and are very much looking forward to having a child together. She's told the girls they're going to have a little brother or sister and they're both very excited.'

If she thought this could pass without controversy, however, she was wrong. First, she was criticised for being pictured smoking and drinking while pregnant. Then she claimed she wanted a 'shotgun wedding' as soon as possible, something that was news to Brian, from whom she was not yet divorced. Kerry was willing to talk about the smoking: 'I am desperately trying to give up smoking but it's really hard and so I do sometimes have a cigarette on the odd occasion,' she said. 'But, as soon as I spark up, I stub it out after just one puff because, being pregnant, I've totally gone off the taste. It makes me feel so ill now and I get enough of that from morning sickness. I've virtually given up. But I'm dead annoyed with myself that I'm finding it so difficult to stop.'

Eventually, Brian decided he would no longer go for custody of the children. It was thus rather unfortunate timing that Kerry now went really public about her past drugs use, as confirmed by her erstwhile friend Michelle Hunter to *News of the World*. 'The first time I saw Kerry take drugs was at a nightclub in 1999,' she said. 'That was ecstasy. Not long after that, I witnessed her take cocaine for the first time in the bathroom at her mum's flat. She scooped it out of a plastic bag with a small coin and sniffed it. I think she offered me some but I said no.'

The two also ran into trouble on a coach trip. 'The police pulled us over,' Michelle continued. 'Kerry panicked, reached into her bra and pulled out her bag of cocaine. She flung it at me and said, "You've got to look after that for us."

'It was like she had her career and didn't want to risk it but I didn't matter. The cops got on the coach and I was terrified. Kerry went to talk to them, explaining that we were on a hen do. Then she came back and I passed the bag over. She just said, "Thanks, mate." That was it, no apology or anything. I was furious. It was only later that I realised just how out of order she'd been. That cocaine was worth about £200 and if I'd been caught I could have got 10 years.

'My two children would have been left on their own and my life would have been ruined. For what? Looking after a friend? But all Kerry cared about that night was getting out of it. I was with her all night and she was constantly in and out of the toilets. She made me wait outside the cubicle so she didn't get caught. It's all Kerry knows. It's very sad. Kerry needs to take a long look at her life, stop lying to her fans and herself and sort herself out for the sake of her kids – or she'll end up dead. Kerry isn't just an occasional user of cocaine. She goes on long binges where she doesn't sleep for days and I'm seriously worried. She's killing herself with cocaine. If she carries on she'll be the next Paula Yates.'

While there was no immediate sign of that, the pregnancy was not going smoothly. Kerry was in and out of hospital with abdominal pains; meanwhile, it was reported that she feared she had brought on attacks of epilepsy by her drug use before she became pregnant. She was then rushed to hospital again when the new Porsche Mark was driving was involved in a crash; fortunately, no one was hurt, but it was a nasty moment.

Matters were made considerably worse when Sue gave an extremely revealing interview to *News of the World*, claiming that not only was it Kerry who introduced her to cocaine and not vice versa, but also that Mark had been Sue's drug dealer, and that was how he and Kerry met. It didn't exactly make for happy families and painted a revealing portrait of quite how out of control Kerry's life had become.

'I'm worried about Kerry – petrified about her,' Sue said. 'I think she'll kill herself with cocaine. She needs help. She can't leave it alone. And getting married to a drug dealer is just my worst ever nightmare. I worry about my granddaughters living in a house with a drug dealer and a girl who has a problem with cocaine.'

Of course, Sue took the drug too, but she was adamant that this had been down to her daughter. 'Kerry introduced me to it,' she said. 'When she was about 16 she was working as a lap dancer in Liverpool and started to earn good money. One night in our local she said to me, "Mum, come to the toilet – I've got something." We both went in and she rolled up a note and laid a line of white powder on the toilet seat. I realised straight away it was cocaine. We had done speed together before but never cocaine. Kerry did it first and then me.'

And, according to Sue, rumours about those epileptic fits were true. 'Kerry and I had been on a huge bender for a few days,' she said. 'We'd done loads of cocaine. But she'd been home and dropped the girls off at school and then she came back to my house. She'd already done a line of cocaine at her home, but she wanted more. I had to phone the dealers and get her drugs because she wouldn't in case she got caught. When it was delivered she went into my kitchen and laid out another line of cocaine, rolled up a note and snorted it up her nose.'

And so the fits began. 'It seemed to go on forever,' said Sue. 'I didn't call an ambulance, I couldn't let her go. White foam was frothing from her mouth and her lips went blue.

'After about five minutes she just lay there in my arms, not moving. I really thought she was dead. I carried her to the sofa and was pleading with her to wake up. When she did I told her what had happened and she was really scared. I thought it might stop her doing coke but it didn't.'

Sue was so alarmed that she got Mark to come round to face the music. 'He sat on my sofa and I told him straight, "She's not doing any more cocaine here,"' Sue said. 'I told him he'd better not have been doing it with her either. He said he wasn't, but I didn't believe him. I knew Mark was a dealer and I'd contacted him to get drugs for me and Kerry. I liked him as a dealer, he was a good laugh. I'd ring and ask him to come a few times a week and drop off £50 bags of cocaine – sometimes for me, sometimes for Kerry, sometimes for both of us. He'd do cocaine with me and we'd have a laugh. He was shagging different birds every night of the week and boasting about it.'

Unsurprisingly, given what she knew about him, Sue was horrified when Kerry became involved with Mark. 'I remember one day last summer and Kez and I decided to get on it. We were at home and the kids weren't there so she said, "Ring up and get some, Mum." I rang Mark and he brought round £50 worth in a clear bag. He didn't come in, just dropped it off. I was drinking Tennants Super and Kerry was on the wine. I'd chop up the coke on the kitchen unit and then we'd both do it. Kerry would do line after line. She wouldn't stop. That night she got me to ring Mark up again even before she had finished the first bag. Then I phoned him about another four times. We had sessions every time the girls were with Brian.

'I saw the attraction instantly. She was seeing Dave Cunningham at the time but she said to me, "I have a thing for Mark, he's really fit." I told her not to go there. He's a drug dealer and that's the last person Kez needed in her life.

'But a few weeks later she came in and was smiling and said, "Guess who I slept with last night, Mum?" I knew instantly it was him. Kerry loves sex when she's on cocaine and she makes no secret of the fact she has a high sex drive.'

Unsurprisingly, this opened yet another set of hostilities, with Max Clifford being called on to defend Kerry yet again. 'Her mum is clearly very sick,' he said. 'She has been dependent on drugs for some time and is strapped for cash. But now Kerry won't give her money for drugs. What happens then is she has to get cash somewhere and tells lies to get paid. We knew this was coming. Papers have been trying to persuade her to do an interview for 18 months.

Kerry is in floods of tears over these claims. She feels hurt, devastated and let down. Kerry is a great little mum.'

In early January 2007, Kerry's divorce from Brian finally came through. She clearly had mixed feelings, remarking on the one hand that it was the best Christmas present she could have asked for and, on the other, that it made her feel as if she'd failed as a mother. 'I'm gutted because my divorce is about to come through,' she said rather sadly. At least she was now free to marry again, while her divorce payout was said to be £1 million.

And the couple didn't waste any time getting wed. With weeks to go before the new baby was due, they tied the knot in Gretna Green in mid-February: Kerry was 26 and Mark 35. The celebration took place at The Mill, an 18th-century listed building with a private chapel, which was lit with candles. In marked contrast to her first wedding, it was all very low key. There was a function afterwards costing just £360, replete with pork pies, pickles and crisps. Meanwhile, the couple prepared to move into a new home in Wilmslow, Cheshire. And the ceremony really had taken place just in time: less than a week after the couple got hitched, Kerry gave birth to her third child, Heidi Elizabeth.

'Mother and baby are doing fine,' reported Max Clifford.

By now, however, Kerry could not move without controversy following in her wake. Brian criticised her publicly for selling her baby pictures, while her sometime friend Jordan was openly hostile towards Mark. 'I think he's a bully,' she said. 'Kerry hasn't even got her own phone. He's taking advantage of how fragile she is. I'm worried about her being the next Anna Nicole. Kerry's too fragile. She should never have married him. I'm saying this because I'm really worried about Kerry and she's a good friend.'

Kerry was not amused. 'When they met, Mark thought Katie [Jordan's real name] was lovely,' she said. 'I'm not going to contact her.' She was also adamant that Mark was a good husband. 'Mark's not a bully. He's treating me a lot better than Brian did. Hopefully, Brian can start finding a new way of getting publicity because using me these days seems to be the only way he can.'

Brian chose to open up about his wedding with Kerry. 'We got married, went back to the castle, I was with my mates, she was with hers, we went to bed at separate times and never had anything,' he said. 'The wedding was a circus, with 400 people. But we had fucking VIP passes for our wedding and special rooms in the castle where VIP guests could stay so they wouldn't have to mix with our families.' He followed this up by adding, 'I was too young to understand what having kids meant. Having a child was like getting a dog.'

Kerry might have brought some of her misfortunes on herself, but it was hard not to side with her on this one. Matters had by now reached such a low that they were barely communicating at all, other than through slanging matches in the papers, each claiming that the other was painting them in the wrong light, and putting their children through goodness knows what in the process.

Kerry lashed out at Brian for the child/dog comparison and she was not alone; he was widely criticised for making such crass and insensitive remarks. 'I can't believe Brian could be so callous and cruel,' she said. 'Our children were born out of love. For him to compare having children to getting a new dog is just cruel and downright evil.'

Few would have disagreed.

But recent events had taken their toll, and no one was more aware of this than Andy McClusky, who had put Atomic Kitten together in the first place. 'I love her to bits but she is definitely a shadow of her former self,' he said rather sadly. 'I just get the feeling that, although she puts on a brave face, Kerry is very unhappy. I worry about her because she is not the girl she used to be. Don't forget, I basically built the band around her. She was so bubbly and happy and had real personality. But now she is a shadow of that girl.'

And, like so many of Kerry's circle, he also didn't think that her second marriage was altogether wise. 'While I don't know Mark and have never met him, the fact that none of her friends and family turned up to her wedding speaks volumes,' he said. 'I think that both Kerry and Brian went at it hammer and tongs way too young and had the kids too early. She just got way too unhappy in Ireland away from her family and friends and with Brian on the road the whole time with Westlife. But I don't think moving back to Warrington has helped her much.'

Nor did the discovery shortly afterwards that her mother

had been falsely claiming benefits support. It was yet another public fiasco which could hardly have helped Kerry's state of mind. Talking to the *Mirror* about the breakdown in her relationship with her mother, Kerry said: 'In spite of everything she has done to me, I get no pleasure from the mess my mother has got herself into,' she said wearily. 'She has made a lot of money by saying nasty things about me to newspapers. And, although I can never forgive the pain she has caused me, she's still my mum. For her to blame Mark is nothing more than I would expect. The fact is an awful lot of people are aware of all the money I have given her as well as the money she has made from the media at my expense. People know what money I have given her.'

As if all this were not enough, in July 2007, Kerry, Mark and Heidi were subjected to an armed raid at their new home, during which one gang member held a knife to Kerry's throat. 'Kerry is in a terrible state,' Max Clifford said the following day. 'When I spoke to her she was in floods of tears and absolutely distraught. My understanding is they held the knife to her throat. It was a terrifying experience. Fortunately, they weren't hurt, but Kerry was held at knifepoint and the robbers threatened to kill them. It was such a horrible thing to happen.' The gang got away with about £150,000 of stolen property, including jewellery, TVs, computers and the couple's car. Understandably, Kerry suffered nightmares for some time afterwards. Meanwhile, the couple's home security was beefed up.

And it seemed there was to be no let up in the drama. More rows followed with Brian over custody arrangements. There were also mutters about a large tax bill looming, indeed, Kerry was eventually made bankrupt although she put this down to cash flow difficulties. Kerry put her worries behind her by going through a second marriage ceremony with Mark – Max Clifford gave her away – before it was revealed that she was pregnant again. Kerry was overjoyed when she discovered she was carrying a boy – but there were still clouds on the horizon. Her tumultuous life was about to get more frenetic than ever.

15

CRAZY IN LOVE

W as it a joke? Had someone finally gone too far? Whoever was behind the decision to call the new reality show starring Kerry and Mark *Crazy in Love* certainly had a sense of irony, for by now events really were spiralling out of control.

Not to mention the couple's love of expensive cars. The couple now had a Ferrari, a Lamborghini, an Aston Martin, a Porsche 911, a Mercedes and a Ducati superbike. Ominously, however, that tax bill remained unpaid. Meanwhile, the publicity shots taken for the new series showed a heavily pregnant Kerry wrapped up in a straightjacket along with Mark. It was felt to be in pretty poor taste.

Shortly before the birth of her fourth child, Kerry and Mark had Heidi christened, before going on for a curry at the Bay Leaf in Padgate, Warrington, shortly afterwards. The budget nature of the affair fuelled rumours about money problems but there was a good-natured air to it all.

The new series debuted to pretty unfavourable reviews, many of which centred on Mark's role in Kerry's life (one of the politer ones pointed out that he had no job and no razor but still managed to drive a Ferrari), and Kerry did herself no favours by allowing herself to be filmed smoking and drinking while heavily pregnant. Meanwhile, rumours of money worries continued to grow. On the one hand, Kerry was said to have spent £1.4 million on the fleet of cars, while, on the other, she was said to be £1.2 million in debt.

Talking of their financial situation, Mark said: 'People say we haven't got any money, but we must have, because, otherwise, how would we have afforded it?' he asked of the car collection.

Max Clifford was diplomatic: 'I have no idea about Mark and his cars. All I know is he makes Kerry very happy,' he said.

Despite her happiness with Mark, Kerry found life so stressful that she had to return for another stay in the Priory. Then, scarcely was she out before she was rushed to hospital amidst fears of pre-eclampsia. Again, it proved to be a false alarm and baby Max was born five weeks early in April.

'Kerry is fine,' said the ever-present Max Clifford. 'She had a natural labour after being induced at lunchtime and Max arrived at 5.42pm. Max is great, he's a little small, but Kerry's baby Heidi was only 4lb 9oz when she was born premature.'

It was only a matter of time before hostilities broke out with Brian again and, this time, when they did, they reached a whole new low. Kerry had said that the early birth had been brought on by the stress of worrying that she would not see her two older daughters again – they had been visiting Brian's parents in Dublin and apparently returned home a few days later than expected.

Brian was incandescent with rage. 'Kerry is a disgusting human being,' he told *News of the World*. 'She manipulates people and plays the sympathy card for every stupid mistake she makes. Me and my family have been put through hell by her stupid games. She uses my two girls as a weapon in her childish games. She is an embarrassment to me, my family and my children. We try to put them into as much of a routine as possible, but it breaks our hearts when the kids quote stuff they've heard from Kerry. "Mummy has to go to the Priory because she's not feeling well" – things like that.'

Kerry responded through the *Daily Star* by kicking him where it hurt – in the career. 'It's very sad,' she said. 'He has done this so many times before. It's the only way he can get publicity any more, which I guess is why he does it. He's got a lot of talent and it's sad that he is using these outbursts to boost his career. When was the last time you ever heard about him when he wasn't attacking me? He has done it so many times and his words are getting stronger and stronger. It's understandable, because it's the only way he can get publicity.'

Brian, however, was far from being the only source of her

worries. There were varying reports about the amount she owed to the Inland Revenue, but it was now out in the open that bankruptcy proceedings were under way. Despite this, another Porsche made an appearance on the driveway, although a spokesperson explained that it was a straightforward swap for the couple's old Aston Martin.

There was no respite wherever Kerry turned. In yet a further blow, as all this was going on, Kerry's mother Susan pleaded guilty to benefits fraud: she had not declared her income from various media outlets while continuing to claim income support and council tax benefit. At the same time, Kerry was devastated when her stepfather Arnold Ferrier died at the age of 78; he was in Texas and Kerry did not manage to get to him in time.

'Kerry was told last week he had been diagnosed with cancer,' said Max. 'She received a call yesterday saying he had taken a turn for the worse. She was desperately trying to get over there to be at his bedside.'

It was quite a blow, especially given the furore around her: Arnold was the closest thing to a father that Kerry had ever had.

Meanwhile, Kerry's finances were going from bad to worse. She had been given ten weeks to pay off a £417,000 tax bill, but £157,000 was still outstanding and couldn't be found. There were attempts to remortgage, but that couldn't be done either, because there was a bankruptcy charge on the house, which prevented her from doing anything. However, her lawyer, Luke Harris, managed to win a final six-week reprieve. Kerry was expecting payments of £472,000 before the end of August, he said, adding, 'She is also strenuously seeking to remortgage her properties. But if the money comes in there is no need. I would ask one final indulgence by the court.'

Worn down by all the stories surrounding them, Kerry decided, with Mark in attendance, to give an interview to set the record straight. For a start, she tackled the thorny issue of the claims that Mark had cheated on her. 'Mark is fed up with all of it,' she declared. 'None of it's true. It's too much. There's even a supposed recording of Mark's voice telling a girl he was only with me for the money. It's gone to a specialist voice analyst to prove it's not him. Mark is my best friend and I've never been more relaxed and happy ever with anyone. We're together 24/7 and we do everything together.'

She then turned to the claims that Mark was a gold-digger. 'Tell me, if Mark was famous and he was in the limelight and earned a lot of money and he then married a woman from the chip shop and was lavishing her with presents, would she be using him?' she asked. 'What's wrong with a woman being the main breadwinner? It's sexism. People have got it in their head that he's bleeding me dry and just after my money. But at the end of the day it's my money. Mark is also managing director of a company and drives me as well, which he gets paid for. And he was involved in my new perfume as well.'

As for her finances: 'It is all under control,' said Kerry. 'I am all fine and not bankrupt. They started calling Mark a gold-digger before the tax bill thing came up.' And Kerry was also still grieving for Arnold. 'He was the last bit of family I had,' she said sadly. 'He wasn't my real dad but he was the only one that was really proud of me and never sold a story. It was a shock, so unexpected and it all happened so quickly. He went to hospital and was told that he had lung cancer and only had until the end of the year to live. But a few days later, I was told he only had two weeks to live. The day before I flew out to see him, he passed away. It was so upsetting.'

Kerry was putting a brave face on it all, but she was bound to have been affected by the continuing drama in just about every area of her life, and so it proved. There were reports of rows with Mark, to the extent that he even briefly walked out, until Kerry persuaded him to return. Then her nanny Gemma threatened to go as well, prompting Kerry to offer a pay rise at a time when her own finances were exceedingly rocky. Her fragility was illustrated in comments made by Max Clifford: 'She is very difficult to manage and I have one person in the office working with her on a full-time basis,' he revealed. 'She can ring us at any time of the day or night, you never know. She's bipolar and needs a lot of help and attention, but I still believe that she is a genuinely good person.'

The battle with the taxman continued: Kerry was granted another two weeks to find the money to pay off the bill. Ultimately, however, it was to no avail and, in late

August, she was finally declared bankrupt after failing to meet the £82,000 bill. Luke Harris said he was 'not in a position to assist further'.

Max Clifford came out fighting: he claimed it should 'never have happened', adding, 'The money is there to cover the bill and they are hoping to get the order annulled next week.' They failed.

Kerry herself was defiant. 'My money just didn't clear on time,' she said. 'I've been told the bankruptcy will be annulled. Our financial adviser, who takes care of all our money affairs, told us that the cash was in place with the court but hadn't been cleared in time. Obviously I'm upset about it but it shouldn't have happened. I've been promised that it will be sorted out this week.'

She was also irritable about the reports concerning the amount she had spent on Mark. 'The stuff about me buying him cars is bollocks,' she said. 'Mark has one, I have one, we have a business one and we have one for the nanny.'

Although the bankruptcy was not annulled, life continued pretty much as usual. For a start, Kerry underwent extensive plastic surgery, paid for and filmed by MTV, in order to return to her previous size-eight figure. 'I'm going to have liposuction because, after four kids, I need it,' she explained before the operation took place. 'I'm also going to have a boob reduction. I'm a GG at the moment and when I take my bra off my nipples are by my feet. I want to be a DD.'

The eight-hour procedure duly took place at the St John and St Elizabeth Hospital in London.

'I feel great,' said Kerry, as she checked out afterwards. 'I'm delighted with the way I look and the way it feels. The results are amazing.'

Perhaps it had also helped to take her mind off recent events, as Kerry certainly looked more cheerful than she had done for a while. Rather puzzlingly, however, given the state of her finances, she then marked her 28th birthday by buying a new car for Mark.

She had other elements to cheer her up as well. She still had her lucrative contract with Iceland, and her new figure was bringing her a great deal of joy. 'I cried at first because I was so shocked,' she said of seeing her new shape. 'I love it. My waist has got smaller, my boobs have been healing. Now I can wear size-10 tops. I couldn't get my tits into them before.' She had done a very sexy photoshoot to show off her new look as well, and was relieved that Iceland approved. 'To be honest, I thought I was going to lose my contract... but the pictures are really nice, classy. I feel sexier, my confidence is back and everyone tells me how amazing I look. I don't think Iceland will want me in a bikini [in the next ad]. That's not why mums go to Iceland, is it?'

However, in the helter-skelter world of Kerry Katona, the calm didn't last for long.

In September, the couple were shaken by the news that Mark might be the father of a 'love child' – it was later proved true – but, given that the child was by now three, there had been no crossover in relationships. 'Even if it's

Mark's kid, it happened a long way before I met him,' she said.

The next crisis followed in late October, when she appeared on *This Morning* with Fern Britton and Phillip Schofield, seemingly unable to concentrate, slurring her words and generally looking a mess. She was there to promote her new show *Whole Again*, and gave a very good impression of someone teetering right on the edge, constantly slurring her words and calling out for Mark.

The presenters noticed it, too. 'You don't seem right to me; you've got the body sorted but your speech is a bit slurred – how are you feeling?' asked Schofield.

'Is it?' replied Kerry, appearing to look alarmed at something behind the camera, before saying that she appeared odd because she was taking prescription drugs. 'I had some [medication] last night, didn't I, Mark? All it is is my medication, I swear. I'm absolutely fine,' she said.

'Have you got rid of one addiction by replacing it with another? Is it alcohol?' asked Fern.

'No, not at all,' said Kerry. 'I'm on holiday in Spain and I'm allowed to have a drink, aren't I? I thought you were trying to find out if I'm an alcoholic now.'

She had been off screen for a matter of minutes before a row broke out. For a start, viewers were appalled that she'd been allowed to go on at all in that condition.

An ITV spokesperson claimed Kerry had turned up late on set, and that the programme-makers had seen 'no cause for concern' at her appearance beforehand.

Kerry herself spoke out. 'I'm not drunk and I haven't got a booze problem. I haven't taken any drugs either,' she said. 'I'm drinking no more than I ever have done before and no more than anyone else. Don't get me wrong, I like a drink and all last week on holiday I was pissed as a fart. But why not? I'm only 28 years old for God's sake. I feel completely stitched up. Why would I go on a TV programme pissed? Do I look stupid? I'll never go on that programme again. I'm extremely annoyed. They're meant to be nice people and I've been interviewed by them many times before. But I've got an illness and they should appreciate that. It's all down to the amount of tablets I'm on for my bipolar disorder.'

But this was one row that was not going to go away.

'There's no way she should have been allowed to do that show. I am increasingly concerned for her,' said Max Clifford to *Newsbeat*.

Whilst maintaining that she had not been drinking before the *This Morning* interview, Kerry was happy to agree that she had enjoyed a drink while on holiday. There was footage of her really knocking it back in Marbella on the couple's recent weekend break; Kerry was pictured downing shots of Martini, Red Bull and vodka, peach schnapps, Sambuca and champagne. 'I'm pissed already and I've only had two glasses of champers,' she said in the interview. 'I used to be able to handle my ale, but last night I was hammered – maybe it's my age.'

It was, in fact, an embarrassment to Schofield and

Britton, both more associated with a laidback style of questioning, rather than a full-on scandal. She was 'obviously very, very angry with us', said Phillip. 'It's a shame that she feels that way because unfortunately she set herself up. The last thing I want to do is to witness a car crash in front of my eyes.'

Mark also felt the need to put out a statement: 'Kerry would like to categorically state for the record that the only thing she drank before the show was cups of tea. Having answered the questions to the best of her ability, Kerry was upset at the insinuation that she was on anything other than the prescription drugs, which she has always been honest about taking.'

For once, Max Clifford, while personally supportive of Kerry, allowed cracks to show. 'In terms of the statement issued by Mark Croft, I've got no sympathy at all,' he said. 'Any journalist would have done exactly the same thing and questioned her about it.'

It then emerged that Mark had lunged at Phillip right after the show, blaming him for allowing Kerry to appear in that state. 'He was jabbing his finger in Phil's face and giving him what for,' said a witness to the scene. 'He was so angry he was frothing at the mouth. It was an extraordinary scene and everyone was standing there with their mouths wide open. He kept saying over and over again that Phil stitched Kerry up and his language was more than a little colourful to say the least. Phil refused to back down, but seemed shocked to be spoken to in that way. Fern was just standing there in a state of astonishment. In the end production staff had to step in to calm things down.'

Indeed, increasingly it seemed the finger of blame was being pointed at Mark. 'If you are concerned about your wife and you are the person who has accompanied her in a car and you notice that her medication is having an effect on her speech, surely you shouldn't bring her into a TV studio,' said Phillip Schofield stoutly. 'In my mind she shouldn't be paraded on television – she should be taken home and loved up and cared for. I think it was irresponsible to put her on the telly and to drive her into us.'

Max Clifford appeared to agree. 'There is no way Kerry should have been allowed to go on the show slurring the way she was,' he said. 'It seems that Kerry and Mark want to do everything themselves. Had I been there, there's no way I would have let her do the show.'

Kerry herself seemed determined to try to shrug it off. 'Schofield was out of order saying I was drunk,' she fumed. 'He is ignorant and arrogant. Why didn't he ask about my condition on air and help explain my slurring was due to my illness and medication? It's discrimination against bipolar people. They asked me why I was slurring and I said it was because of my illness and because of my prescription medication. But they ignored the fact. It was discriminatory to anyone with my condition. I would take action against him – but I want to see what happens first.'

There was a further, real blow when it emerged that she had now split from Max Clifford. 'I gave her away in

Italy and have almost been a surrogate dad to her,' said Clifford. 'I've been there through the depression and drink and drugs. I just wish her health and happiness.'

The unspoken assumption seemed to be that Kerry wasn't taking enough advice from him. And, if that were not enough, the nanny walked out. There was drama everywhere she turned.

It transpired it was actually Kerry who severed the link with Max, apparently angry that he had voiced concerns about her drinking. 'She has asked that I no longer represent her,' said Max. 'Reluctantly I have agreed and I wish her all the health and happiness. I think the world of her and wish her every success.'

In an earlier interview with *Heat* magazine, Max had made his feelings clear. 'All I can say is that, from knowing Kerry as well as I do, I don't personally believe she is in a good place at the moment. What people who are around her tell me makes me increasingly worried. People around her are telling me that she is drinking more and more, earlier and earlier. All I can say is that Mark was happy for Kerry to go on *This Morning* which says a lot. Mark is at the centre of Kerry's life and so you can't overestimate the effect he has on her life. She loves him to bits and therefore he has an impact on everything she does.'

In November, Kerry decided to make a statement about her drinking and it appeared to confirm what everyone had feared. 'I am an alcoholic,' she said. 'I have never admitted this before and I know it is a battle I will have to face for the rest of my life. By coming forward I hope it will help others. During my worst drinking bouts I'd easily knock back ten to fifteen shots of vodka or peach schnapps. I can get through days without having a drink but it's hard. I can never promise myself or my family that I can beat this addiction but I will try very hard.

'I take one day at a time now. I haven't been to AA because I believe I'm controlling the drink not the other way around. I believe I have my illness under control because my first priority is to my children and husband. I remember my mum Sue taking me to the pub and I would fall asleep under coats. I don't want mine to remember me in the same way.'

The couple were adamant, however, that drink had had nothing to do with her shambolic appearance on *This Morning*. 'The night before the interview Kerry only had one drink – a vodka and Red Bull at around 11pm while she was filming another TV show,' said Mark. 'Her slurring was purely down to the medication she took later that night for her bipolar disorder. There has never been a picture of Kerry coming out of a club legless. She'll say to you, "I'm getting pissed," but people who don't know Kerry label her as a major drunk who is out every night. Medical people have asked her, "How much do you drink?" and she's said, "I don't have one drink or two but I intentionally go out to get pissed."'

It had certainly been a tumultuous year, finished off by a DNA test that proved that, as expected, Mark was the father of a three-year old son by an ex-girlfriend. He appeared to wish for only limited involvement: 'I'm not ready to have another son brought into my life,' he said. 'While it sounds nasty, I've got my family. I don't want anything to do with him, though financially I'll do as best I can to help out. It's not up for discussion.'

Paradoxically, however, at the end of the most incident-packed year of what had been a very incident-packed life, Kerry was looking better than she had done in years. It wasn't just as a result of the surgery, either: she had started working out with a personal trainer, and the pounds fell off. Her trainer was former *Coronation Street* star Scott Wright, and she was looking so well that friends joked she was now telling Mark to pull himself together. She appeared as besotted with her husband as ever, however, and happy with him too.

The year ended with yet more reported spats with Brian, none of which looked likely to come to an end in the short term, more reports of rows with Mark and more speculation about her future. But Kerry stood up to it all, managing to cope with a string of crises just one of which might have felled a lesser woman. At the time of writing, she was preparing for another reality-television show. What doesn't destroy you makes you stronger. Kerry still has a fair way to go.